FOOTBALL'S MIS-DIRECTION WING-T

WITH MULTI-POINTS OF ATTACK

Carl O. Gentry

COACHES CHOICE

ISBN: 1-57167-124-2
Library of Congress Catalog Card Number: 97-65487

Book Layout: Antonio J. Perez
Diagrams: Antonio J. Perez, James Hunt
Cover Design: Deborah M. Bellaire
Front cover photo: Bill Wood
Back cover photo: Jack Newsom

Coaches Choice Books is an imprint of: Sagamore Publishing, Inc.
                                            P.O. Box 647
                                            Champaign, IL 61824-0647
                                            (800) 327-5557
                                            (217) 359-5940
                                            Fax: (217) 359-5975
                                            Web Site: http//www.sagamorepub.com

DEDICATION

To my family...
My wife, Mary;
My children—Billy and his wife, Anita;
Marcy and her husband, Allen Baysinger;
Tom and his wife, Kris.
To my grandchildren—Travis, Haley, Adam
Clayton, Samuel; and Zachary.

ACKNOWLEDGMENTS

The 38 teams of players whose super effort and dedication to the game of football made all the success happen. . . I salute you.

The 38 coaching staffs who taught the skills and motivated those teams to reach their highest potential. . . I salute you.

Thanks to the parents and the fans for your support. There is nothing like a "packed house" where people are "hanging from the rafters" to motivate a super-performance from the young men on the field. . . *I salute you.*

CONTENTS

Dedication 3

Acknowledgments 4

Preface 7

Chapter

1   The Concept 9

2   Method of Operation 13

3   Blocking Schemes and Techniques 27

4   Staff Assignments 47

5   Play Selection and Introduction to the "Packages" Section 51

6   The Fullback Package 55

7   The Counter (CX) Package 71

8   The Counter Boot Package 85

9   The Sweep Package 91

10   The Sweep Boot Package 119

11   The Option Package 127

12   Wing-T Supplement 133

     The Author 151

PREFACE

In January of 1996, I retired after 38 consecutive years of head football coaching. During those 38 years, the teams I had the honor of coaching won 305 football games and averaged eight wins per season. This book is a tribute to all of those players, coaches and their families who applied the effort and dedication to "make it happen."

The primary purpose of this book is to share with you information about an offense that we used the past 22 years—one which played a major role in our success. I hope you find some interest or value in the content of this book that will help in your football program.

After 22 years of running the same type of offense, I literally collected a "mountain" of material; consequently, in this book only the major aspects of the Mis-direction Wing-T offense are covered. If you wish further information, please feel free to contact me.

B. G.

CHAPTER 1

The Concept

In 1974, after 16 years of running three different offenses, I decided to adapt the Wing-T of the 1950s and 60s to a more up-to-date view that suited our way of thinking. As a direct result of that decision, our "three points of attack" philosophy off of the Wing-T Mis-Direction series was developed. Logically, we named this offensive scheme, "Mis-Direction Wing-T With Multi-Points of Attack."

The fundamental concept of this scheme is to produce three possible points of attack on each snap of the football in a true mis-direction style of offense. The basic intent of this offense is to control defensive pursuit and cause hesitation of linebackers.

In order to more clearly demonstrate the three points of attack concept, the following basic sets and their descriptive points are diagrammed and discussed.

The Counter Break

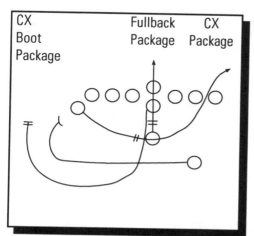

Left Formation
√ 18" splits in the line and off
the ball maximum.

Diagram 1-1

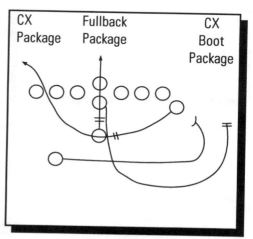

Right Formation
√ 18" splits in the line and off
the ball maximum.

Diagram 1-2

Fullback—is in a three-point stance with his helmet six feet from the QB's butt. He will dive every snap and will not bend his course to avoid the QB.

Halfback—is in a two-point stance behind the tackle with his toes two feet deeper than the FB's heels. He will get a wall position on the defensive end for the counter boot play.

The Wing—is in a two-point stance with his toes in 1/8 of a turn. He assumes a position with a 12" split from the outside foot of the tight end. He will run a 1/2 moon course and come to the QB for the ball or a fake.

The Quarterback—will pivot out of the FB's path and will either fake or give the ball to him (as called in the huddle). Next, the QB will run a 1/2 moon course and either give or fake the ball to the counter back and continue his counter boot course. The counter boot is always "run first" intent.

<table>
<tr><td>*Left Fly Call*
√ Same plays as right call.</td><td>*Right Fly Call*
√ Same plays as left call.</td></tr>
</table>

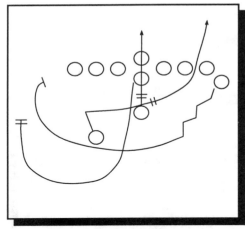

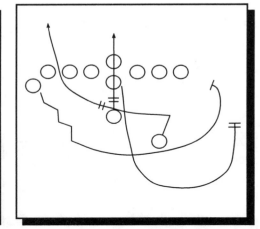

Diagram 1-3   **Diagram 1-4**

Left Double Call
√ Same plays as left formation
and right fly formation.
√ Three formations to left.

Right Double Call
√ Same plays as right formation
and left fly formation.
√ Three formations to right.

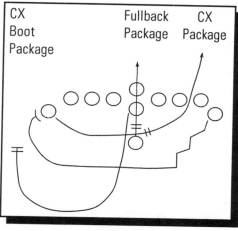

Diagram 1-5

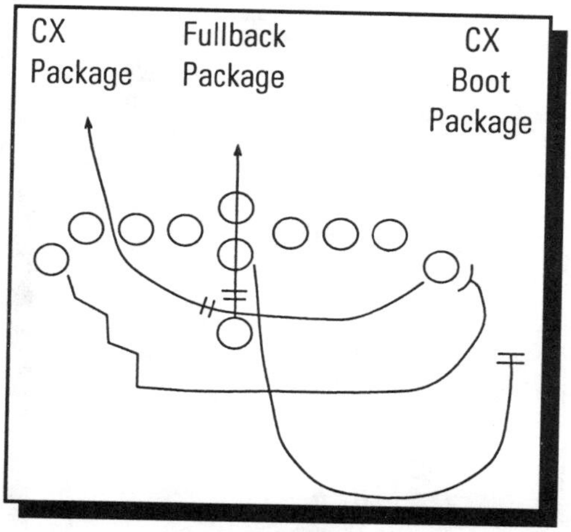

Diagram 1-6

All plays are mirrored. The backs are not flip-flopped. Our snap count is in cadence in order to coordinate the 1-count full-speed fly. The fly man must be at his halfback position at the snap.

The Sweep Break

Left Formation Call

Right Formation Call

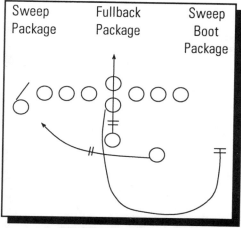

Diagram 1-7

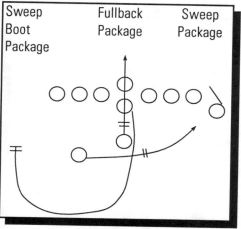

Diagram 1-8

The fullback dives as in the counter break and either gets the ball or a fake. The halfback will run his sweep break and get the ball or fake. The wing blocks on sweeps and is a receiver on the boots. The quarterback initially either gives or fakes to the fullback, next gives or fakes to the halfback, and finally continues his 1/2 moon course to run his boot or fake it.

Right Fly Formation Call
√ Same plays as left call.

Left Fly Formation Call
√ Same plays as right call.

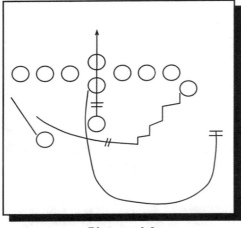

Diagram 1-9

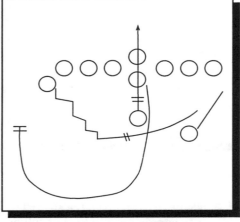

Diagram 1-10

Left Double Call
√ Same plays as left call and right fly call.
√ 3 sweep formations left.

Right Double Call
√ Same plays as right call and left fly call.
√ 3 sweep formations right.

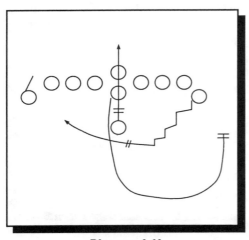

Diagram 1-11

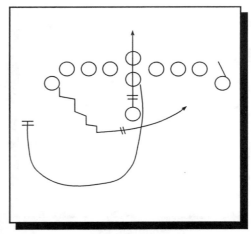

Diagram 1-12

CHAPTER 2

Method Of Operation

Holes and Labeling of Plays

We employ a standardized system for identifying the holes and labeling the plays. This system helps clarify where each player must go on a play and what his responsibilities are on that particular play. Diagram 2-1 illustrates how we designate the holes—even numbers to the right and odd numbers to the left.

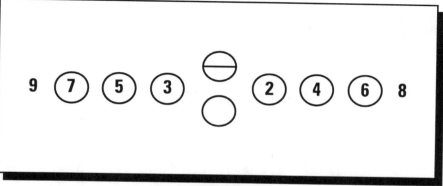

Diagram 2-1

- The formation called first: Right, Left Fly and Right Double. Right Double means that the left wing will fly, which puts us in a right formation at the snap. The flip side of these formations are: Left, Right Fly and Left Double.

- The first digit is the series break.

- The second digit is the hole to be attacked.

- A word added means special action or a blocking change.

- Example: "Right 28 Sweep." Right formation; 20 series; the hole is 8 sweep.

The Snap Count Method

Our count system is in cadence, so that we may coordinate the one-count fly series.

> "READY"—We never snap on ready.
> "SET"—First count.
> "HIT"—Second count.
> "HIT"—Third count.
> "HIT"—Fourth count.

We also mix first sound snaps by using the word, "GO." We do not make a "READY" call if we are going on first sound. We cannot snap on "GO" if it is a fly play. We also can make a live call before the "READY" call.

Series Calls (First Digit)

- 20 Series means that the fullback will dive (Diagram 2-2).

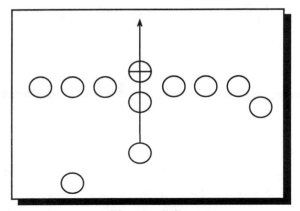

Diagram 2-2

- 30 Series means:

    a. On counters, the fullback plugs away from the hole (Diagram 2-3).

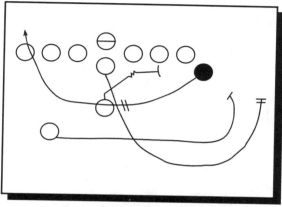

Diagram 2-3

    b. On sweeps, the fullback will kick out or escort the ball; the playside guard will not pull (Diagram 2-4).

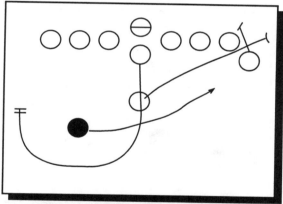

Diagram 2-4

• 40 Series means that the fullback will carry the ball on special plays, and the blocking scheme will remain the same as for 20 series.

    a.   40 Series Sweep (Diagram 2-5).

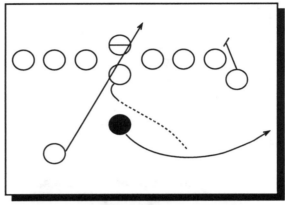

Diagram 2-5

    b.   The Slant-Option (Diagram 2-6).

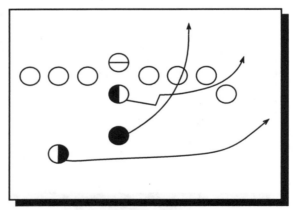

Diagram 2-6

c.   The Wham (Diagram 2-7).

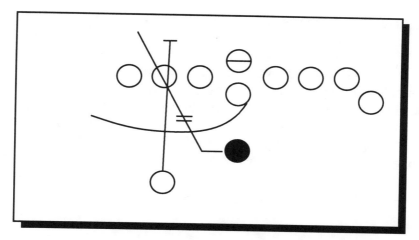

Diagram 2-7

- The 50 Series is the same as the 30 Series for the fullback and the same as the 20 Series for the line; hence, 20 and 30 equals 50. Diagram 2-8 illustrates an example—the Right 58 Base Sweep.

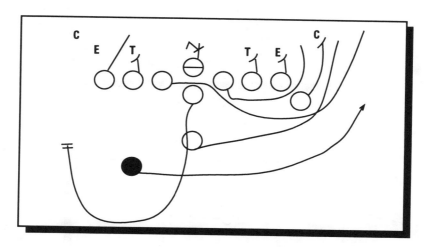

Diagram 2-8

Teaching the Backs

Proper courses are vital to this offense. Smooth connections on the "fake and take" must be made without hesitation or change in courses, in order to produce a "quick take-off" operation on each and every snap. At first, no ball is used when we are teaching the backfield breaks. We explain that everyone is getting the ball. Once an acceptable level of production is achieved, a ball is then used. Initially, the backs are divided into two groups—a quarterback and fullback group and a halfback and wing group to accomplish the fundamental moves. Next, the whole backfield is brought back together to initially practice the backfield breaks at learning speed and then progress to full speed. The spacing strap is used to get our land marks.

- The Counter Break and Progression (Diagrams 2-9, 2-10 and 2-11)

  a. Right call.

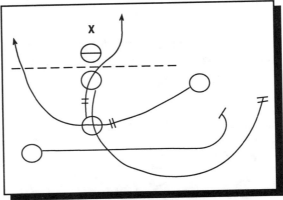

Diagram 2-9

  b. Left fly call.

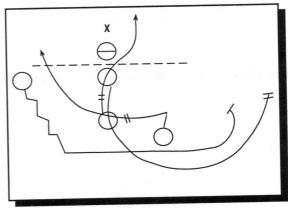

Diagram 2-10

c. Right double call.

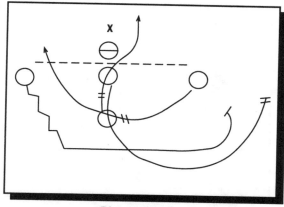

Diagram 2-11

d. Repeat from left formations.

Coaching Point: At this point, the team should be able to run the fullback trap, the counter and the counter boot from all six formations.

- The Sweep Break (Diagrams 2-12, 2-13 and 2-14)

a. Right call.

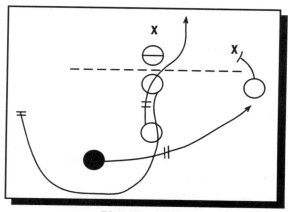

Diagram 2-12

b. Left fly call.

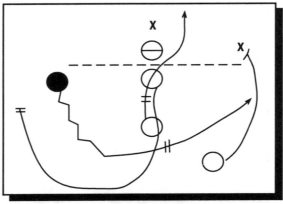

Diagram 2-13

c. Right double call.

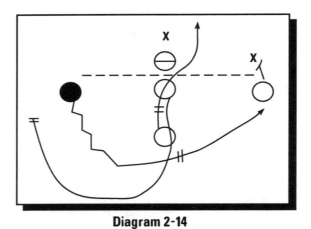

Diagram 2-14

d. Repeat to the left.

Coaching Point: At this point, the team should be relatively proficient at running
the wide fullback trap, the sweeps and the sweep boot from
all six formations.

Fundamental Techniques for Each Backfield Position on the Counter Break

- The Counter Break from the right call—repeat to left (Diagram 2-15)

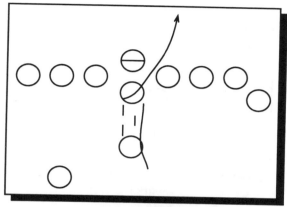

Diagram 2-15

a. The fullback steps first with his foot opposite the hole. He will receive the ball or the fake on his second step. He will plant and cut on his third step. He will cover the ball or the fake with both forearms until he clears the linebackers. He will sell the carry on fakes and try to get tackled.

b. The wingback (Diagram 2-16).

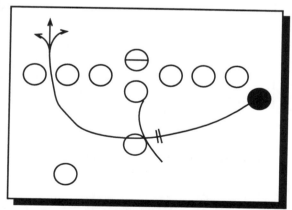

Diagram 2-16

The wing will point his inside toe on a half-moon path. He will take a course through the fullback's shoulder pads, come to the quarterback, and continue his course to cut upfield between the tackle and the tight end with his shoulders parallel to the line of scrimmage as he enters the hole. If he is carrying the ball, he will run to daylight. If he is faking, he will make some cuts and sell the counter.

c.   The halfback (Diagram 2-17).

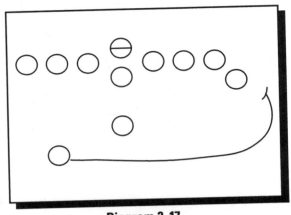

Diagram 2-17

The halfback will sprint flat out with full speed to beat the quarterback and get an "outside-in" blocking position on the first, unblocked opponent.

d.   The quarterback (Diagram 2-18).

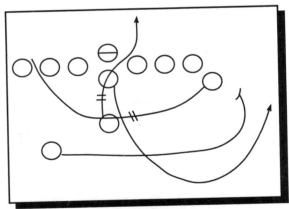

Diagram 2-18

The quarterback will pivot to avoid the fullback's path. He will bring the ball to the fullback's navel and will give it to him or extract it. He will continue as the wing comes to him. He will either place the ball on the wing's navel or will rub the wing's navel with his open hand. He will then continue the half-moon circle and will either fake the counter boot or execute the counter boot with the "run first" philosophy.

- The Counter Break from the left fly formation (Diagram 2-19)

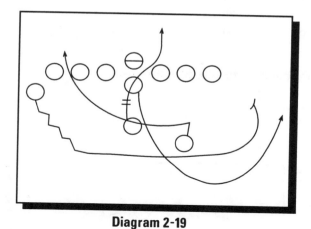

Diagram 2-19

a. The actions of the fullback will not change from the right call.

b. The halfback will take a large step toward the outside foot of the tight end, grab grass with his outside hand as he slides the inside foot up and then cut the half-moon path. He will now be in the same position as from his wing path.

c. The wing will fly full speed on the one-count allowance and proceed to get his wall-block position.

- Counter Break from the right double call (Diagram 2-20)

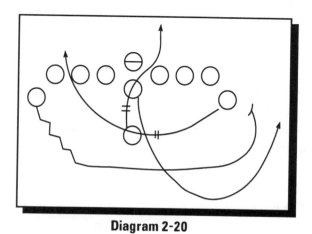

Diagram 2-20

It is not necessary to practice the double formation, since all of the techniques are already mastered on the other calls.

Coaching Point: Repeat from the left call, the right fly call and the left double call.

Fundamental Techniques for the Sweep Break

- Right formation (Diagram 2-21)

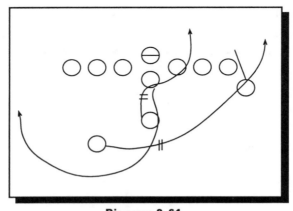

Diagram 2-21

a. The fullback will work on a wide-cut path through the outside foot of the guard.

b. The halfback will take a slight upward path and will take the ball on the sweep or take a fake. If he gets the ball, he will read the blocking leverage by the kick man for the cut. If he does not get the ball, he will sell the sweep.

c. The quarterback will open as usual for the fullback give or fake. He will continue to the halfback and will either give the ball to the halfback and fake the sweep boot or will fake the sweep and execute his boot with "run first" philosophy.

d. The wing will block on the sweep and release, after a block fake, on the bootleg.

- Sweep Break on the left fly formation (Diagram 2-22)

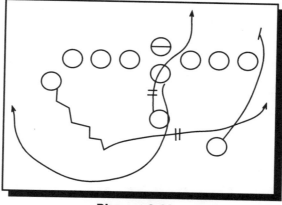

Diagram 2-22

a. The actions of the fullback and the quarterback will not change from the right formation.

b. The halfback will either block at the outside foot of the tight end or will fake-block and release for the boot.

c. The wing will fly one count to his halfback position and will carry on the sweep or fake the sweep on the boot play.

- The Sweep Break on the right double formation (Diagram 2-23)

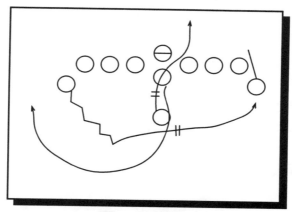

Diagram 2-23

No need exists to practice the fundamentals on the double call, since all of the attendant techniques are from the other formations and have already been practiced.

CHAPTER 3

Blocking Schemes and Techniques

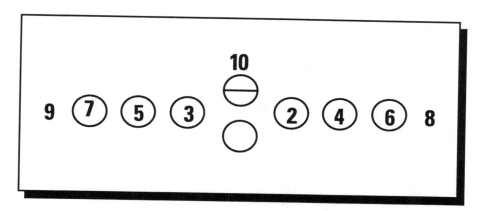

We number our player positions with even numbers to the right and odd numbers to the left. Guards are the 2 and 3 holes, tackles are the 4 and 5 holes, tight ends are the 6 and 7 holes, and the wide holes are 8 and 9. The right foot of the center is the 0 hole, while his left foot is the 1 hole. When we call plays, the last digit is the hole to be opened.

We employ two primary blocking schemes: the "POWER SCHEME" and the "DOWN SCHEME." If we do not add a block call after the hole number, then we will automatically employ the power scheme. If a blocking word is added to the play, then we will change to that type. In other words, the power scheme is our basic blocking scheme, while with the down scheme is the alternate. We also employ some special letter and word calls to change the blocking scheme.

The Power Scheme

- We will double-team the first downman inside of the hole called

    a. Hole man.

        √ Lead down on the downman on the first inside teammate.
        √ If no downman is present, then block the first inside linebacker (BAB).
        √ If there is no inside linebacker or if the defensive placement will not allow you to BAB (block across backer), then influence by either pulling and trap the first outside man or step up, make slight contact and block away (SUBA).

b. The first lineman inside of the hole called:

√ Post, a downman on.
√ If no downman on, then lead down on the first downman inside.

c. All other assignments are predetermined on each play.

Coaching Point: It sounds complicated, but it really isn't. Let's take the 7 hole cx as an example (Diagrams 3-1, 3-2, 3-3 and 3-4):

√ vs. 52 (double man on tackle) HOLE MAN—Lead.

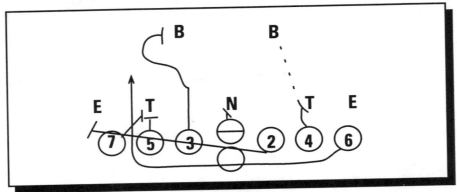

Diagram 3-1

√ vs. 43 (double man on guard) HOLE MAN—BAB.

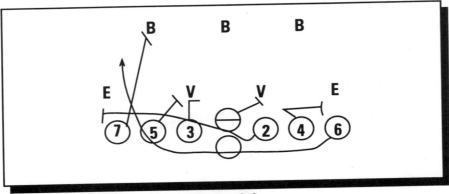

Diagram 3-2

√　vs. Split 4 (double man on guard) HOLE MAN—BAB.

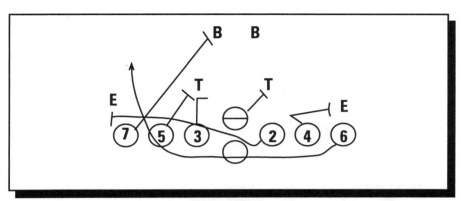

Diagram 3-3

√　vs. Split 4; the defensive end will not allow the holeman to BAB, so the holeman will SUBA (step up, chip, and block away—influence). HOLEMAN—can't lead, can't BAB; so SUBA.

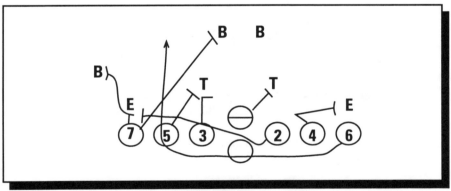

Diagram 3-4

Coaching Point:　To repeat:
7 hole is called.
　＊ Holeman—lead, BAB, SUBA/influence.
　＊ First inside—post, lead.
　＊ Second inside—base, post.
　＊ Others—predetermined on 7 counter hole.

The Down Scheme

- We can take care of certain kinds of defensive stunting and shooting by linebackers in our power scheme by sealing and scooping, but there are times when we are forced to "break up the double" and go to the down scheme. The down scheme assignments are a simple block down on the first person inside.

  Coaching Point: Again, the 7 hole counter can be used as an example (Diagrams 3-5, 3-6, 3-7):

  a. vs. 52.

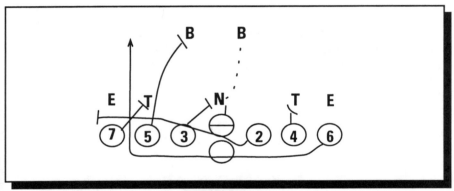

Diagram 3-5

  b. vs. 43 (the playside guard will color call if he cannot block down on the middle linebacker).

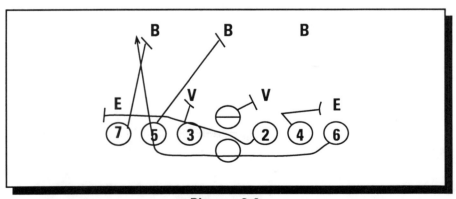

Diagram 3-6

c.   vs. Split.

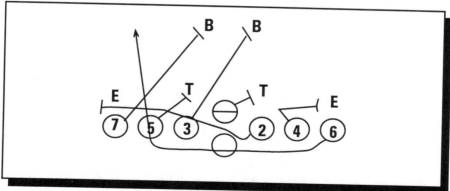

Diagram 3-7

d   vs. Eagle.

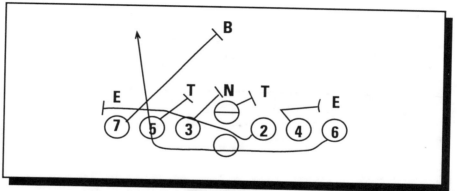

Diagram 3-8

- Special blocking calls

a.   G call (Diagram 3-9). The word "George" means it is a guard call.

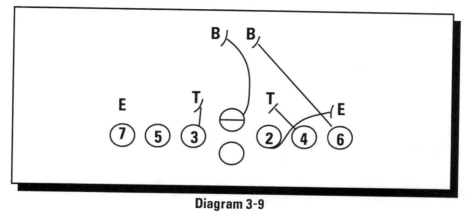

Diagram 3-9

b. GT call (Diagram 3-10). Means both the guard and the tackle are involved (George and Tom).

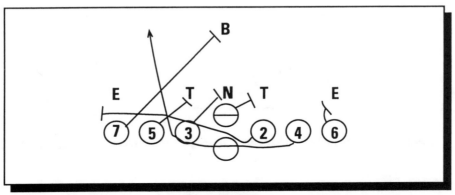

Diagram 3-10

c. Fold call (Diagram 3-11). On the base scheme, assignments are switched when the playside guard has a hardship block.

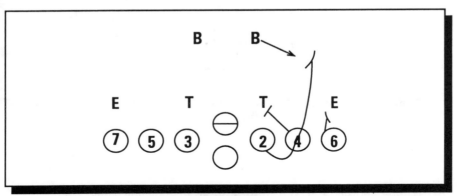

Diagram 3-11

d. Color call (Diagram 3-12). On a down scheme, a color is called by the guard when he cannot block down.

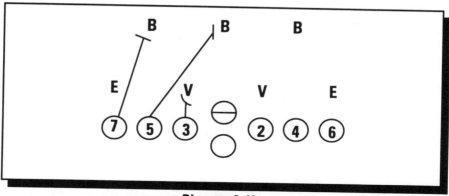

Diagram 3-12

e. S call (Diagram 3-13). Inside switch; the opposite of a fold call.

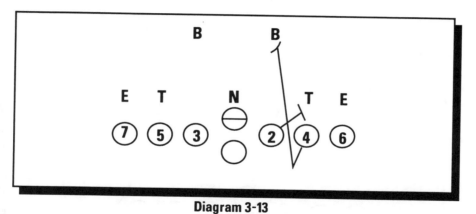

Diagram 3-13

f. Base call (Diagram 3-14). The offensive lineman blocks the man on him.

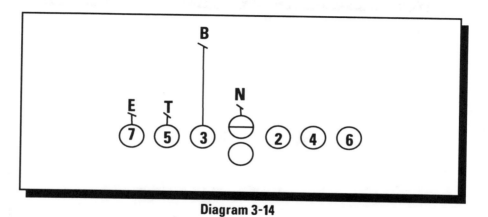

Diagram 3-14

g. Zone call (Diagram 3-15). Enables the guard and tackle to pick up both the downman and the linebacker.

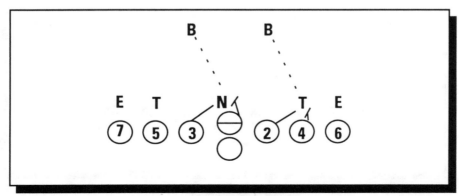

Diagram 3-15

h. Combo call (diagram 3-16). Again, this call enables the tight end and the wing to pick up both the downman and the linebacker. Combo is the opposite of a zone call.

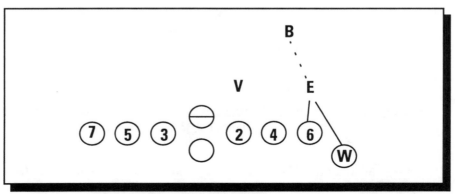

Diagram 3-16

- Blocking techniques

  a. Base (inside, on, outside) (Diagram 3-17).

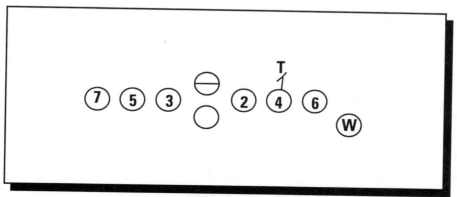

Diagram 3-17

The blocker should attain leverage on his initial contact, get his pads under his opponent, drive him off the line, finish him off with his hands and "keep the glue" on his man.

  b. Post/lead (power block) (Diagram 3-18).

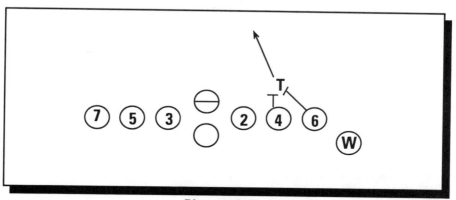

Diagram 3-18

√ The post man (the inside man) employing the shoulder nearest the lead man drives the defender upfield, using his shoulder and forearm with a neck lock to the inside.

√ The lead man, employing the shoulder nearest the post man, drives the defender on a 45-degree angle inside using a shoulder and forearm with a neck lock to outside.

c. Trap block (inside-out block) (Diagram 3-19).

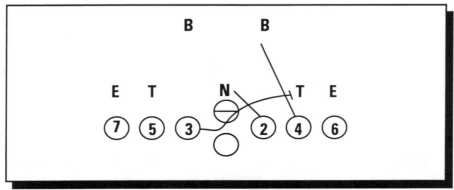

Diagram 3-19

The blocker jerks his inside arm hard, turns his inside foot parallel (he does not step), cross-over steps, and gets up in the hole. The blocker contacts the defender with his shoulders square to the sideline and employs leverage—he gets under the defender's pads, drives him outside, then turns him deep.

d. Kick block (blocking the contain man).

√   The playside guard (Diagram 3-20).

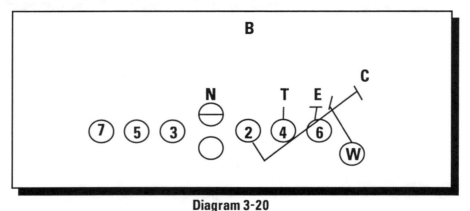

Diagram 3-20

The playside guard gets width and depth on his first step. The blocker uses a crossover step and works up into the hole and traps the contain man. If the contain man over-closes, the playside guard should log him by placing his leverage outside and basing him up.

√ Fullback (on 30 series) (Diagram 3-21) .

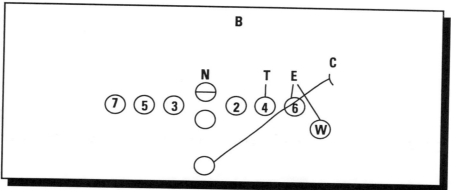

Diagram 3-21

The fullback gets the angle through the inside foot of the tight end. The fullback works up into the hole to get a trap block. If the contain man over-closes, the fullback should place his leverage outside and base him up.

e. Down block (the first opponent to inside).

√ The blocker uses his near-shoulder on a man who is not penetrating. The principles of the lead block are followed (Diagram 3-22).

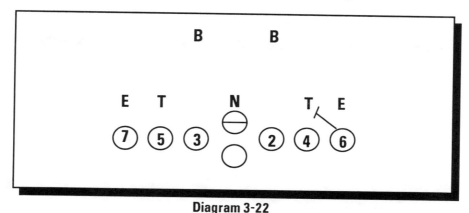

Diagram 3-22

√   The blocker uses his far-shoulder on a defender who is penetrating by placing his helmet under the defender's chest and executes the far-shoulder contact and drives down (Diagram 3-23).

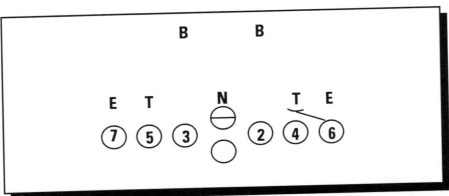

Diagram 3-23

f.   BAB block (block the first across linebacker) (Diagram 3-24) . The blocker takes a path through the hip of the tackle to meet the coming linebacker. The blocker employs the down block fundamentals.

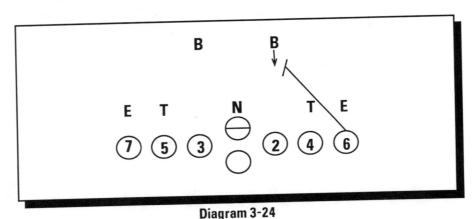

Diagram 3-24

g. Cutting off the Linebacker (Diagram 3-25). (Get the correct position.) Take the escape path. As soon as you are clear, upturn toward the run lane, square up and lock up on the linebacker with the hands block.

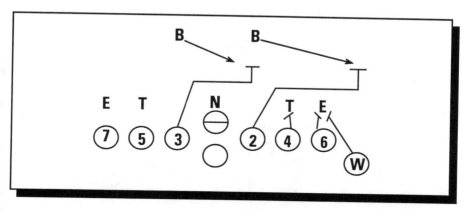

Diagram 3-25

h. Escort block.

√ Tight end escort on the counter (Diagram 3-26). Stepping for width and depth, the tight end runs with his pads down. He keys the helmet of the trapping guard. If the guard's helmet is inside, the tight end squares up and gets through the hole with his eyes upfield. He takes inside first, his second choice is on and last choice is to take the outside.

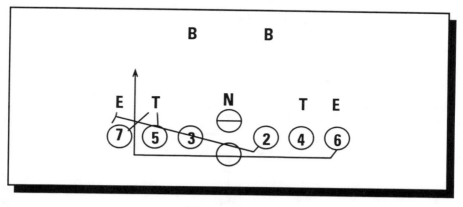

Diagram 3-26

√   Sweep escort by the off-guard (Diagram 3-27). The off-guard pulls as if he is trapping. He must beat the fullback and get depth. He keys the playside guard's helmet. If his hat is inside, then the off-guard squares up, and gets through the hole (inside, on, outside). If the playside guard's helmet is outside, he then escorts outside.

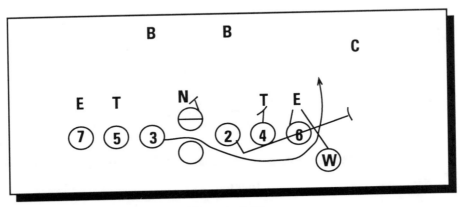

Diagram 3-27

i. Seal block (the closing of the hole left by a pulling lineman, principally, on sweeps and sweep boots). When sealing, the blocker turns his foot, crosses-over, lunges and sprints his backside shoulder behind the butt of the second man over. Continuing to sprint, the seal blocker forces the defender to go behind him or through him. The seal blocker does not allow the defender to cross his hat.

√   Sealing the 52 (Diagram 3-28).

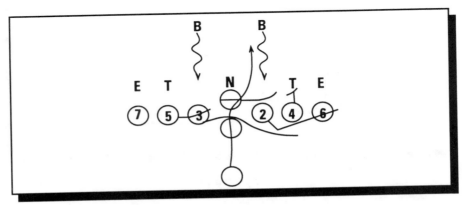

Diagram 3-28

√ Sealing the 43 (Diagram 3-29).

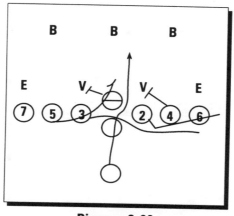

Diagram 3-29

√ Sealing the Split (Diagram 3-30).

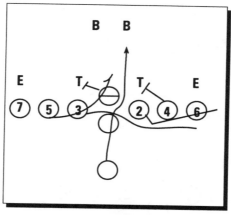

Diagram 3-30

√ Sealing the Eagle (Diagram 3-31).

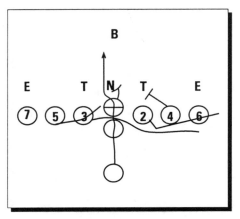

Diagram 3-31

j. Reach block (outside, on, inside).

√ Wing reach (Diagram 3-32). The reach block is used when the wing or the halfback is asked to get outside leverage on the contain man. The blocker must sprint toward the sideline and get a square-up position on the contain man. The blocker then locks up with the contain man, uses the "hands block" on the defender's chest for control. The blocker moves his feet laterally and keeps the "glue" on until help arrives.

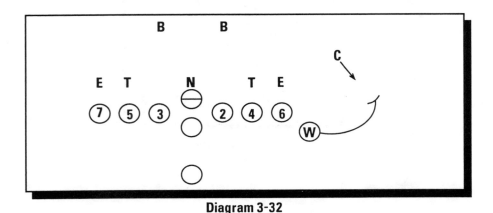

Diagram 3-32

√ Reach block for the halfback (Diagram 3-33).

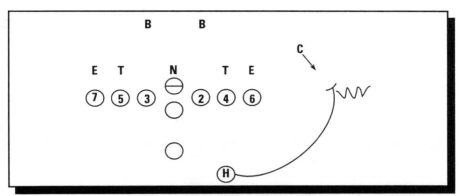

Diagram 3-33

k. The wall block.

√ The halfback and the fly back employ a wall block on the counter boot. The halfback/wingback must sprint at full speed to get past the quarterback's path. They must key the first unblocked opponent. They get a position two yards outside of the defender, then work in under control and lock the defender up using the hands technique. The blocker's primary objective is to prevent the defender from getting to the quarterback's boot path (Diagrams 3-34 and 3-35).

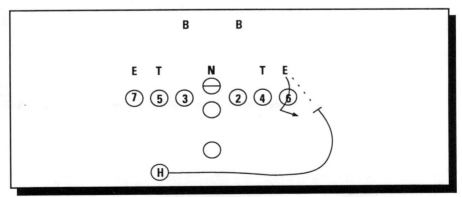

Diagram 3-34

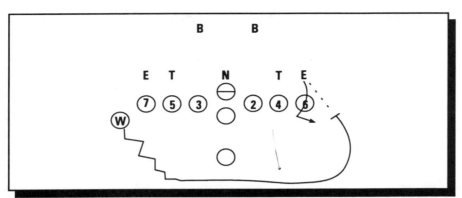

Diagram 3-35

√ The playside guard on the sweep boot. On the sweep boot, the playside guard is called the "wall guard." His job is to get an outside-in position on the first unblocked opponent and prevent him from going to the quarterback. The wall guard must pull deep in a circle path. He should be a full three yards deep at a point directly behind the tight end's pre-snap alignment. He must locate the defender and adjust his position until he can get his hands on the defender, lock him up and keep him inside (Diagram 3-36).

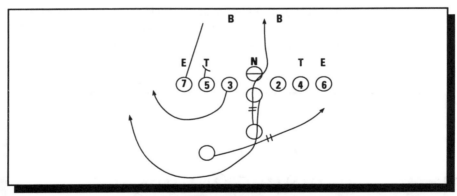

Diagram 3-36

l. The fold block. The fold block is a part of the base blocking scheme. A fold block is used when a blocker is disadvantaged.

√ The playside tackle must execute the down block quickly and must drive the man so that the blocker's heels are clear of the guard's path on the fold.

√ The playside guard is the fold man. In a fold block, he must take a large side step for depth and width and then crosses over up into the hole, keeping his shoulders parallel to the line. He must anticipate the movement of the linebacker and move to a lock-up position, using the hands technique in order to gain some degree of outside leverage (Diagram 3-37).

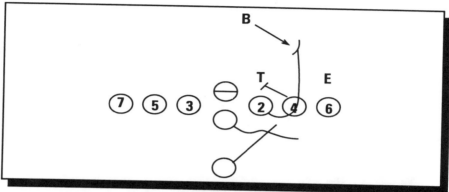

Diagram 3-37

m. The color block (Diagram 3-38). In the down blocking scheme, a few defensive alignments pose a disadvantage for a blocker.

√ The playside guard is disadvantaged because he may not be able to down block the middle linebacker on the 43 alignment. As a result, he should call a color to his tackle and switch assignments. In this situation, the guard has base, while the tackle has the linebacker.

√ The playside tackle, on a color call, will block the play guard's man instead of blocking down.

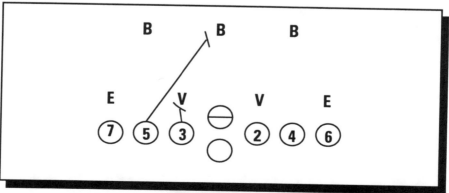

Diagram 3-38

CHAPTER 4

Staff Assignments

Teaching and implementing the Mis-direction Wing-T with multi-points of attack offense can be handled with coaching staffs of various sizes.

- Ideally, a four-man staff is appropriate (Diagram 4-1).

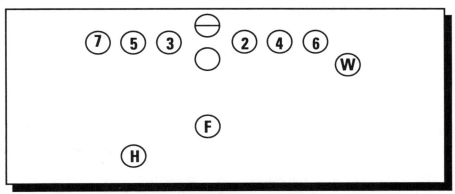

Diagram 4-1

a. Phase 1 breakdown

√ Interior line
√ Tight ends
√ Halfback and wing
√ Quarterbacks and fullbacks

b. Phase 2 breakdown

√ Centers and guards—interior coach
√ Tackles and tight ends—tight ends coach works the integration between the tackles and tight ends.
√ Backfield group—quarterbacks and fullbacks coach and halfbacks and wings coach.

c. Phase 3 breakdown

√ Front seven—interior coach and tight ends coach
√ Backfield group continue

d. Phase 4 breakdown

    √ Centers, guards and tackles—interior coach
    √ Tight ends and backfield—blocking coordination between halfbacks, wings and tight ends; the pass attack

e. Phase 5 teamwork (Diagram 4-2). The tight ends coach handles the scout defense and coaches the tight ends.

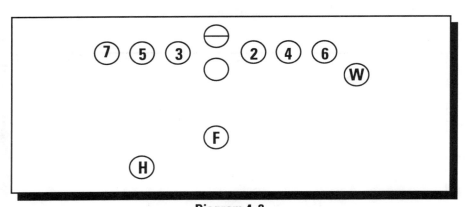

Diagram 4-2

- A three-man staff (Diagram 4-3).

a. The line coach can handle the front seven nicely, due to the double tight situation.

b. In teamwork sessions, the halfback/wingback coach takes the scout team, while the quarterback/fullback coach handles the backfield.

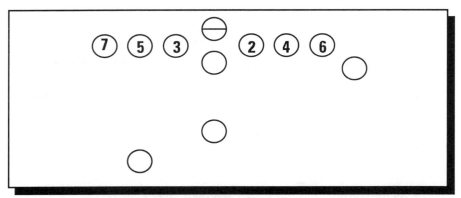

Diagram 4-3

- A two-man staff (Diagram 4-4).

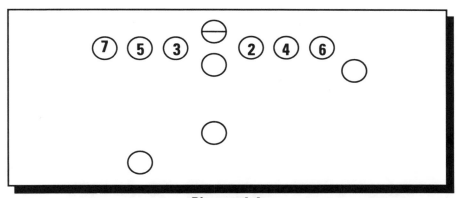

Diagram 4-4

Coaching Point: A two-man staff is often particularly suitable for small high schools and/or junior varsity and freshmen level programs.

CHAPTER 5

Play Selection and Introduction to the "Packages" Section

Play Selection

A bad play cannot be called in this offensive system as long as the play caller adheres to the principle of "keep 'em mixed thoroughly." The key point to remember is that the play caller must not establish tendencies that his opponents can feed on. Among the personnel who are responsible for helping select and send a play into the game are the following

- If sufficient personnel are available, two individuals involved in play selection are located in the press box—a play caller and a spotter. The play caller should be the line coach. He should work closely with a press box spotter who should observe the defense and its reactions, changes and tendencies. The press box spotter should chart this information and pass it along to the play caller "right now."

- The sideline phone man should get the play to the QB in a timely fashion, via messenger or signal.

- The sideline chart man should record the formation, the play, the down and distance, the field position and the result.

- The "Take Off Coach" is responsible for getting players out of their stances on the snap. He should note all eleven hats and motivate those who are even a hair late. The snap count should start a "feeding frenzy" on the part of the offense.

At least six guidelines should affect a coach's philosophy of selecting plays:

- Mix the plays and the formations in all situations of down and distance and field position.
- Do not "fall in love" immediately with a play that gains well.
- Do not file divorce proceedings on a play that does not gain.
- Mix flies equally and mix formations equally; furthermore, mix formations and flies to the wide and short sides of a field equally.

- Remember that boots and counters are excellent short yardage and goal line calls, as long as a team has established the philosophy of "run first" on boots.
- Mix run and pass in short yardage situations and mix run and pass in long yardage situations.

Introduction to the "Packages" Section

Note: All plays are diagrammed to the right only. The reader must flip them to the left.

- Right formations

  a. Right (Diagram 5-1).

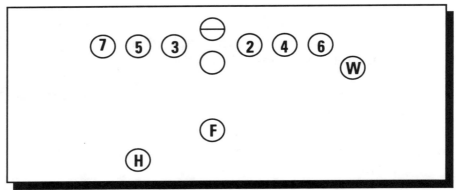

Diagram 5-1

  b. Left Fly (Diagram 5-2).

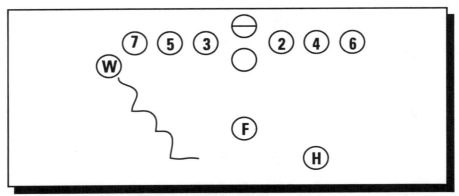

Diagram 5-2

c.   Right Double (Diagram 5-3).

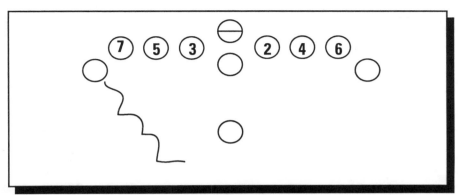

Diagram 5-3

- All plays against the 52 defense are diagrammed first and then carried on through the 43, the Split, and the Eagle.

   a.   The 52 defensive alignment (Diagram 5-4).

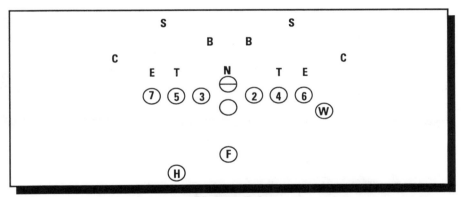

Diagram 5-4

b. The 43 defensive alignment (Diagram 5-5).

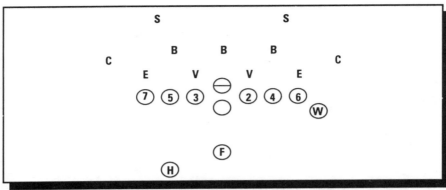

Diagram 5-5

c. The Split defensive alignment (Diagram 5-6).

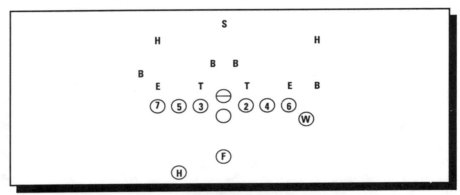

Diagram 5-6

d. The Eagle defensive alignment (Diagram 5-7).

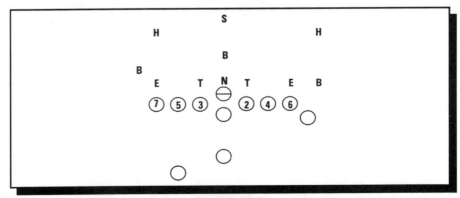

Diagram 5-7

CHAPTER 6

The Fullback Package

In our three points of attack concept, the fullback is the focal point. Given the fact that the fundamental philosophical basis of the Mis-direction Wing-T with multi-points of attack offense is to control pursuit, then the middle attack must be emphasized. This approach forces the defense to "check and take or eliminate" the fullback on every snap. The fullback must cover and conceal the ball with both arms until he clears the linebackers. When the fullback is faking, he must proceed, exactly, as if he has the ball. He must "sell the carry" to the defense. The fullback package is the backbone of our mis-direction offense and is the primary reason that the remainder of our attack is able to produce excellent results.

We prefer a small, quick fullback. The small fullback needs less of a running lane crease. The blocking ability of our fullback is last on the list of our requirements for a fullback.

Blocking Rules and Position Symbols

C	The Center
PG	Playside Guard
BG	Backside Guard
PT	Playside Tackle
BT	Backside Tackle
PE	Playside Tight End
BE	Backside Tight End
FB	Fullback
HB	Halfback
WB	Wingback
QB	Quarterback

- 22 Trap

  a. Right 22 Trap vs. the 52 defense (Diagram 6-1).

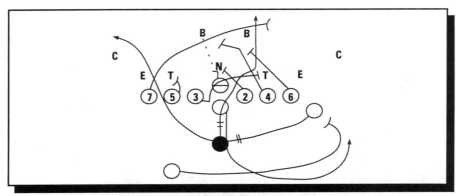

Diagram 6-1

PG	(Hole called) lead, BAB, SUBA/influence.
PT	BAB/combo.
PE	BAB (block across backer).
C	Away, post.
BG	Trap first downman past the center.
BT	Base, linebacker.
BE	BAH (block across hole).
FB	Dive, receive ball, cover ball, cut behind trapper, get around the BAB and upfield. Make the trapper hurry.
LH	Get wall position on first unblocked for cx boot.
WB	Fake counter carry. Sell it.
QB	Give to FB. Sell counter; sell counter boot.

  b. Left Fly 22 Trap vs. the 43 defense (Diagram 6-2).

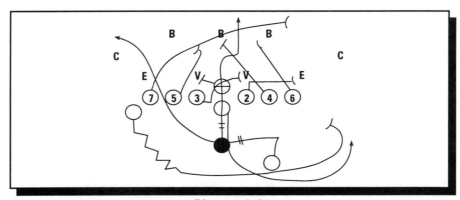

Diagram 6-2

c. Right Double 22 Trap vs. the Split defense (Diagram 6-3).

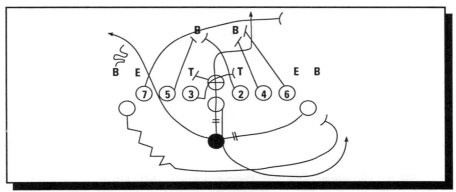

Diagram 6-3

d. Right 22 Trap vs. the Eagle defense (Diagram 6-4).

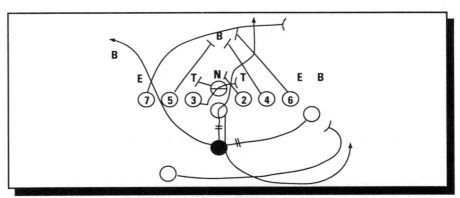

Diagram 6-4

• Special fullback plays vs. the 52 defense

a. 22 Dive (Diagram 6-5).

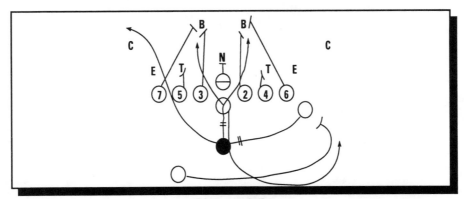

Diagram 6-5

PG	Base.
PT	Base.
PE	BAB.
C	Base the nose man the way he wants to go.
BG	Base.
BT	Base.
BE	BAB.
FB	Key nose man's helmet; take ball and cut away from nose man's helmet.
Others	Same as 22 Trap.

b. 22 Dive double S vs. the 52 defense (Diagram 6-6).

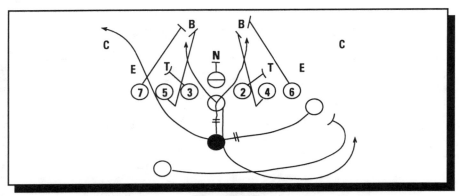

Diagram 6-6

PG	Block out; drive him out quickly.
PT	Step in and get up on linebacker.
PE	BAB.
C	Same as dive.
BG	Block out; drive him out quickly.
BT	Step in and get up on linebacker.
BE	BAB.
Others	Same as 22 Dive.

c. 22 Dive SOS—SOS means that the Guards step out to sideline (Diagram 6-7).

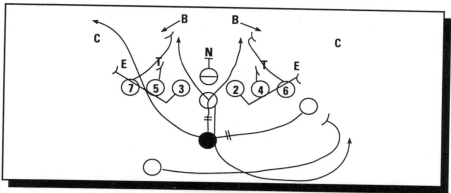

Diagram 6-7

PG	Pull out and trap the defensive end.
PT	Base.
PE	Dig the linebacker.
C	Same as 22 Dive.
BG	Pull out and trap the defensive end.
BT	Base.
BE	Dig the linebacker.
Others	Same as 22 Dive.

d. 22 Trap "backdoor" vs. the 52 defense (Diagram 6-8).

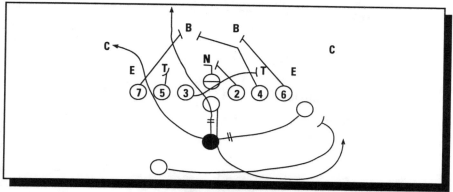

Diagram 6-8

All assignments are the same as 22 Trap except:

BE	BAB.
FB	Take ball and cut away from hole.
BT	Has the key block. Keep hole open.

- 22 Trap-Toss

    a. Right 22 Trap-Toss vs. the 52 defense (Diagram 6-9).

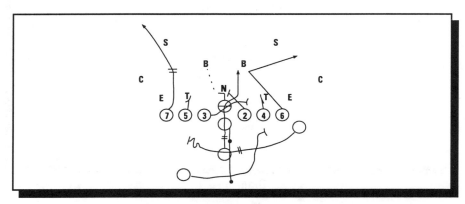

Diagram 6-9

Coaching Point: The trap-toss controls the backside linebacker.

PG	Lead.
PT	Base, out.
PE	BAB, lets LB hit him, break out to daylight.
C	Away, base.
BG	Trap two area.
BT	Base, out.
BE	Escape step, upfield looking for toss at 5 yards. If "pump," break to flag looking for ball outside.
FB	Super fake the 22 trap. Run into linebacker.
HB	Wall path, break up to block DE.
WB	Counter path, break and block DE.
QB	Take ball to FB, pop the ball to BE at five yards deep. If he is covered, pump and drop and look from BE to PE for "feed off."

    b. Left Fly 22 Trap-Toss vs. the 43 defense (Diagram 6-10).

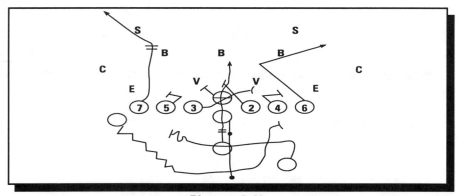

Diagram 6-10

c.   Right Double 22 Trap-Toss vs. the Split defense (Diagram 6-11).

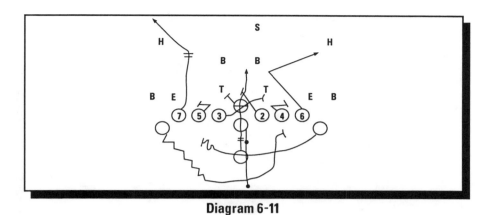

Diagram 6-11

d.   Right 22 Trap-Toss vs. the Eagle defense (Diagram 6-12).

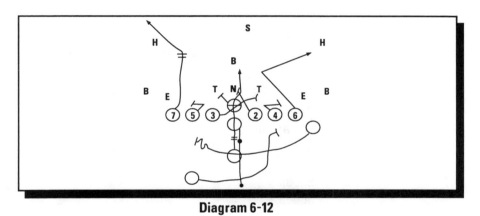

Diagram 6-12

Coaching Point: 22 Trap-Toss "PUMP" may be called in the huddle
and the toss would be faked.

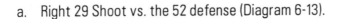

- 29 Shoot (controls the defense to tight end/halfback side of the formation)

   a. Right 29 Shoot vs. the 52 defense (Diagram 6-13).

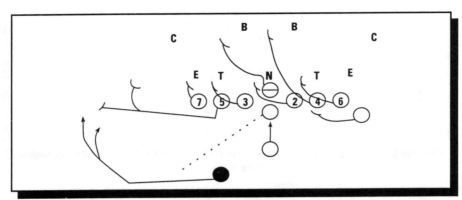

Diagram 6-13

Coaching Point: We call this play when our tight end can base block the defender on him and the contain man is off the line of scrimmage.

PE	Base.
PT	Pull at full speed, slightly upfield toward the sideline. Reach-block the contain man or wall him out into the sideline.
PB	Scoop.
C	Scoop.
BG	Scoop.
BT	Scoop.
BE	Scoop.
WB	Scoop.
QB	Get the ball to the HB right now.
HB	Sprint flat full speed until the ball arrives. Do not wait for the ball. Stretch the defense. Cut daylight.
FB	Fake the dive.

b. 29 Shoot vs. the 43 defense (Diagram 6-14).

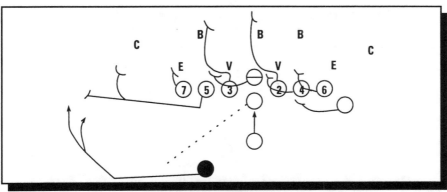

Diagram 6-14

c. 29 Shoot vs. the Split defense (Diagram 6-15).

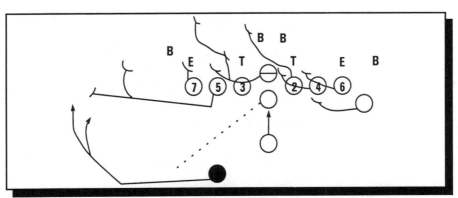

Diagram 6-15

d. 29 Shoot vs. the Eagle defense (Diagram 6-16).

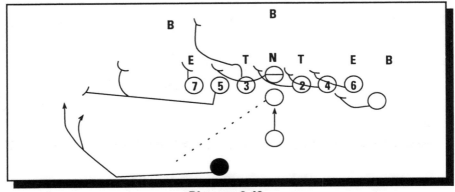

Diagram 6-16

- 22 Trap Shoot-Toss

    a. Right 22 Trap Shoot-Toss vs. the 52 defense (Diagram 6-17).

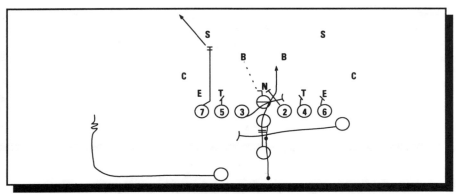

Diagram 6-17

All assignments are the same as for the 22 Trap-Toss except:

HB   Shoot out until a point 12 yards wide is reached, then
            turn up and hang just behind the line of scrimmage.
QB   Sell the trap, hit the TE; if open, if not, drop and check
            flat and flag.
WB   Block the backside DE.

Coaching Point: The toss to the TE is still the number one choice.

    b. Right 22 Trap Shoot-Toss vs. the 43 defense (Diagram 6-18).

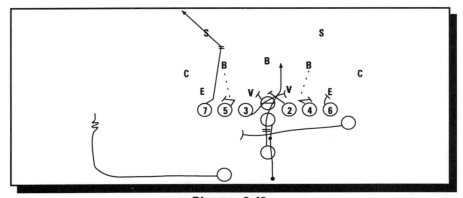

Diagram 6-18

c.   Right 22 Trap Shoot-Toss vs. the Split defense (Diagram 6-19).

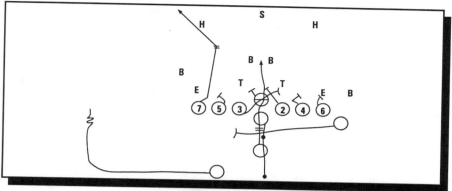

Diagram 6-19

d.   Right 22 Trap Shoot-Toss vs. the Eagle defense (Diagram 6-20).

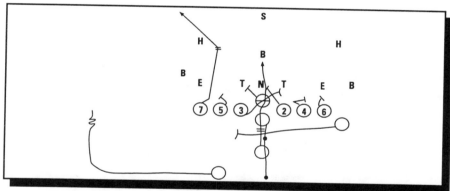

Diagram 6-20

- Shoot 23 Trap

  a. Right Shoot 23 Trap vs. the 52 defense (Diagram 6-21).

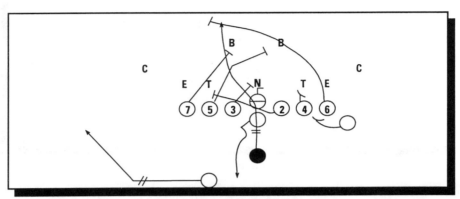

Diagram 6-21

All assignments are the same as for the 23 Trap except the backfield action.

Coaching Point: Fake the shoot and run the trap to side of shoot action. Keep in mind that some linebackers like to run to shoot action.

  b. Right Shoot 23 Trap vs. the 43 defense (Diagram 6-22).

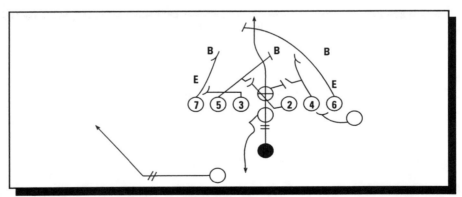

Diagram 6-22

c.   Right Shoot 23 Trap vs. Split defense (Diagram 6-23).

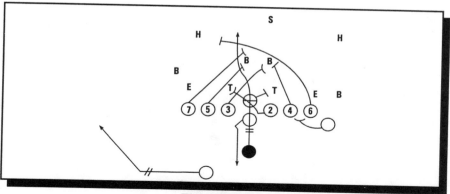

Diagram 6-23

d.   Right Shoot 23 Trap vs. the Eagle defense (Diagram 6-24).

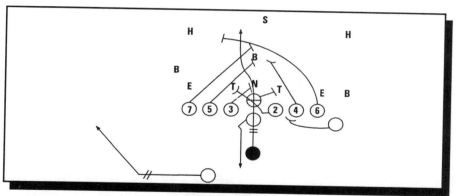

Diagram 6-24

- 24 Trap Down.

  This play is the "wide" fullback trap. We always run the 4 and 5 hole traps out of the sweep break, in order to influence the outside portion of the defense and to keep them from compressing.

a. Right 24 Trap vs. the 52 defense (reverts to 2 hole, if playside guard is uncovered) (Diagram 6-25).

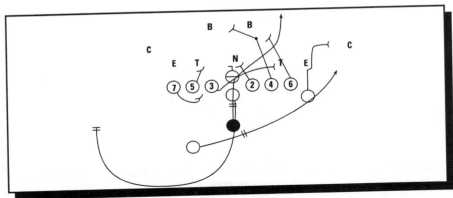

Diagram 6-25

Coaching Point: The down blocking scheme is always called on the 24 and 25 traps.

PT   (Hole called) Down.

PG   Down (make color call for switch with PT if necessary).

PE   BAB.

C   Away.

BG   Trap first down man past the PG.

BT   Scoop, seal the ball.

BE   Scoop, seal the PT hole.

FB   Same steps as in 22 trap, except make a sharp cut to get around the down block on the defender on the PG.

QB   Give the ball to the FB. Sell the sweep. Sell the sweep boot.

HB   Sell the sweep.

WB   Influence/chip the DE and wall out the contain man.

Coaching Point: If the 24 trap is called and the defense shows up in the 52, then we automatically execute the 2 hole trap.

b. Left Fly 24 Trap vs. the 43 defense (Diagram 6-26).

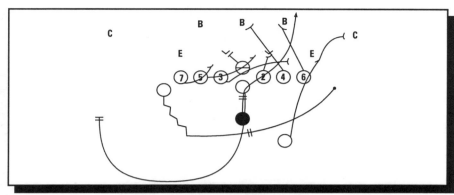

Diagram 6-26

Coaching Point: Color call by playside guard since he cannot down block middle linebacker.

c. Right Double 24 Trap vs. the Split defense (Diagram 6-27).

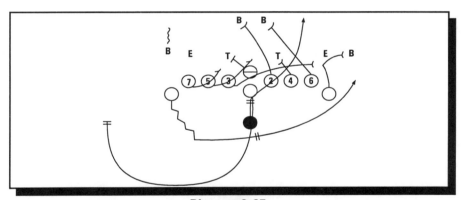

Diagram 6-27

d. Right 24 Trap vs. the Eagle defense (Diagram 6-28).

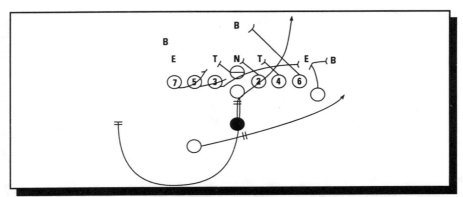

Diagram 6-28

CHAPTER 7

The Counter (CX) Package

The counters have been our leading average per-carry plays. Statistically, the counters were number two on the list of most called plays, with the fullback trap being number one. The counter has produced positive results in all situations of down, yardage and field position, including the "red zone" and the goal line. The counter play to our left has always out-gained the one to the right. We hypothesize that this situation is either the result of our blockers' right-handedness or dominant side or a by-product of the strong side placement of defensive personnel to our right.

In the Mis-direction Wing-T offense, the counter is a "basic" play, whereas in most offenses it is an occasional play. Frankly, the Mis-direction Wing-T offense involves more counter plays than almost any modern offense, although it appears that many of the current one-back offenses are countering more than ever before.

- The 27 Counter

    a. Right 27 Counter vs. the 52 defense (Diagram 7-1).

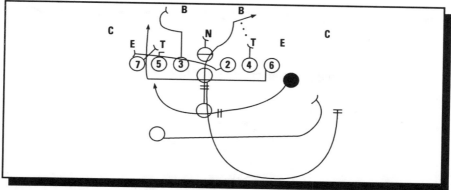

Diagram 7-1

PE	Lead, BAB SUBA (hole called).
PT	Post, lead.
PG	Base.
C	Base, away.
BG	Trap or log first color.
BT	Seal, base.
BE	Escort through hole. Read the hat of the trapper to cut up or go wide.
FB	Sell the trap.
HB	Fake the wall block.
QB	Sell the fullback trap; give to counter back; sell the counter boot.
WB	Catch the escort man. Read trapper's hat for cut.

b. Left Fly 27 Counter vs. the 43 defense (Diagram 7-2).

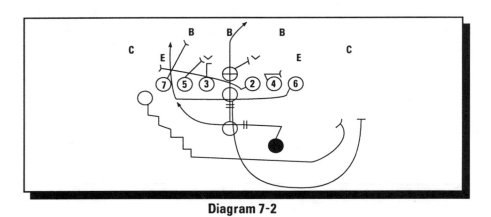

Diagram 7-2

c. Right Double 27 Counter vs. the Split defense (Diagram 7-3).

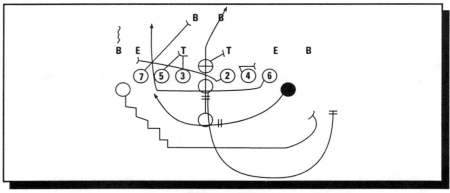

Diagram 7-3

d. Right 27 Counter vs. the Eagle defense (Diagram 7-4). (Note: We usually make a down call vs. the Eagle).

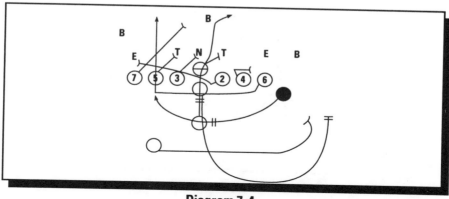

Diagram 7-4

When teaching the counter, the following teaching points should be emphasized:

√ Holeman blocking rule progression

    a. Lead, when tackle is covered (Diagram 7-5).

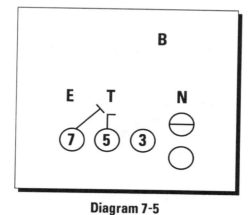

Diagram 7-5

b. BAB, when tackle is uncovered (Diagram 7-6).

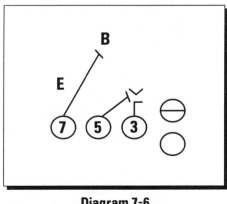

Diagram 7-6

c. SUBA, when defensive alignment will not allow a BAB (Diagram 7-7).

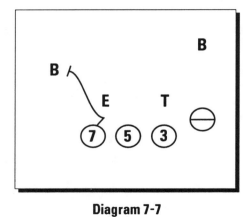

Diagram 7-7

√ The down blocking scheme call for the 27 counter play. Huddle call is "Right 27 cx Down."

    a. Down vs. the 52 defense—actually a pair of zone blocks (Diagram 7-8).

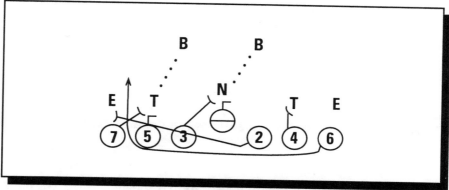

Diagram 7-8

    b. Down vs. the 43 defense. PG makes a color call to PT (Diagram 7-9).

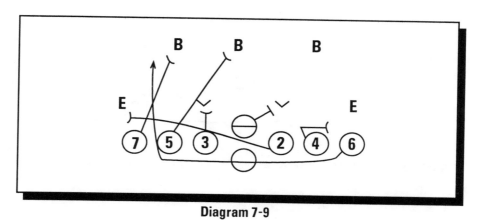

Diagram 7-9

c. Down call vs. the Split defense (Diagram 7-10).

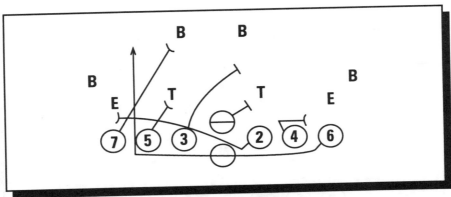

Diagram 7-10

d. Down call vs. the Eagle defense. SUBA is shown when DE will not allow a BAB by either PE or the hole man (Diagram 7-11).

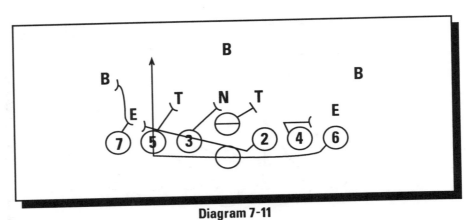

Diagram 7-11

√ We go to the down scheme when the seal blocks are not successful and when the defense presents major blitzing.

√ If the defensive end chases the counter successfully, then we call the 30 series on the counter and plug him with the fullback. The chase of the counter has never been a major problem since we are extremely quick on the count, and we get in the hole right now and attempt to "catch" the escort man (Diagram 7-12).

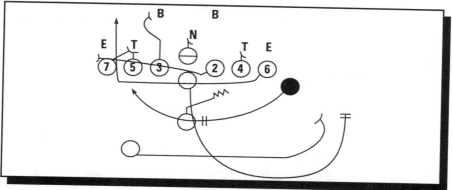

Diagram 7-12

• The 27 Counter Lateral Call.

The purpose of this call is to prevent the closing nature by the defensive end and the contain man. Draw the defense in to the counter and then pitch the ball outside.

a. Right 27 Counter Lateral vs. the 52 defense (Diagram 7-13).

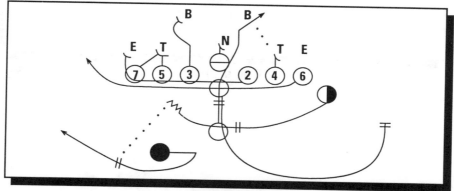

Diagram 7-13

The blocking schemes are the same as for the 27 counter except:

BG	will always log the DE.
BE	will escort the play wide.
CX Back	will run the counter until he approaches the play tackle. He will break down his feet and make a controlled pitch.
HB	will turn the inside foot and take two steps, plant and face the line as he pivots back for depth. He will get a lateral position and "hang" until the ball is pitched. He will carry with "wide" intent while reading the block of the escort man.

Coaching Points:

√ We will also call a "Base Scheme."

√ If we feel that the backside defensive end will chase and interfere, then we will run this play using the 30 series and plug him with the fullback.

b. Left Fly 27 Counter Lateral vs. 43 defense (Diagram 7-14).

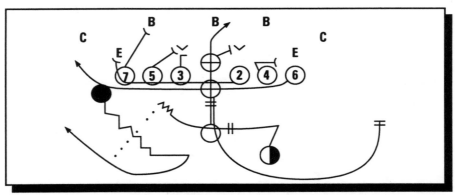

Diagram 7-14

c. Right Double 27 Counter Lateral vs. the Split defense (Diagram 7-15).

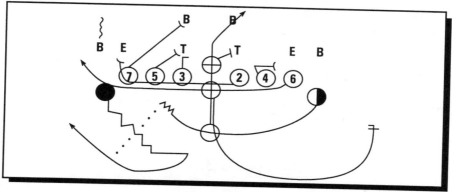

Diagram 7-15

d. Right 27 Counter Lateral vs. the Eagle defense (we like the down call vs. the Eagle) (Diagram 7-16).

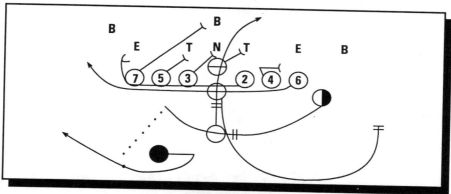

Diagram 7-16

- The GT (guard and tackle) Call on the counter play.

  We add the GT Call to the down scheme. We also run GT from 30 series to avoid the "conflict" between the fullback and the pulling tackle.

  a. Right 37 Counter Down GT vs. the 52 defense (Diagram 7-17).

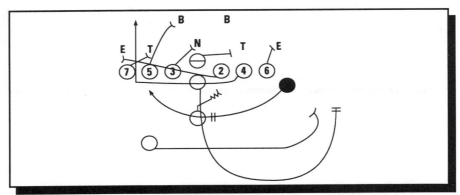

Diagram 7-17

  b. Left Fly 37 Counter Down GT vs. the 43 defense (Diagram 7-18).

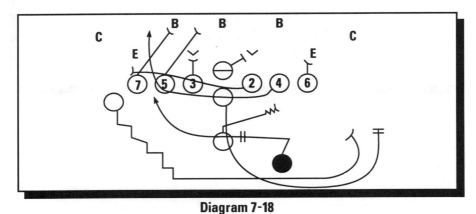

Diagram 7-18

c. Right Double 37 Counter Down GT vs. the Split defense (Diagram 7-19).

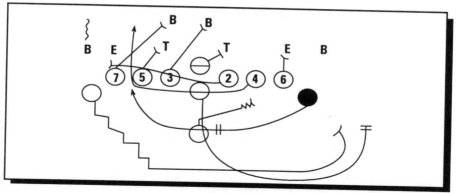

Diagram 7-19

d. Right 37 Counter Down GT vs. the Eagle defense (Diagram 7-20).

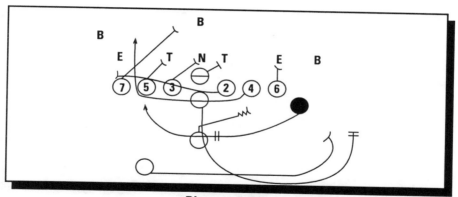

Diagram 7-20

- The "TOM" Call.

  This call on the counter play means that we want the tackle to be the trapper and the playside guard will block away on the down scheme. This call is very effective against stunting and blitzing defenses.

a. Right 37 Counter Down Tom vs. the 52 defense (Diagram 7-21).

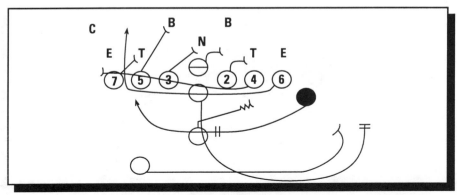

Diagram 7-21

b. Left Fly 37 Counter Down Tom vs. the 43 defense (Diagram 7-22).

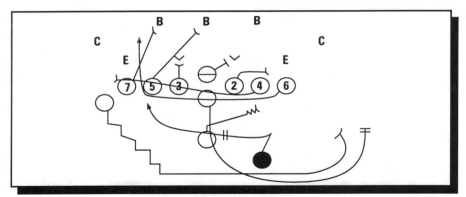

Diagram 7-22

c. Right Double 37 Counter Down Tom vs. the Split defense (Diagram 7-23).

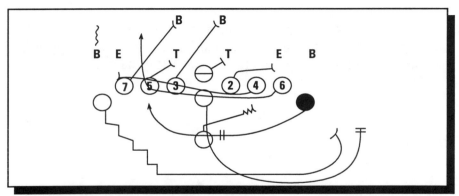

Diagram 7-23

d.   Right 37 Counter Down Tom vs. the Eagle defense (Diagram 7-24).

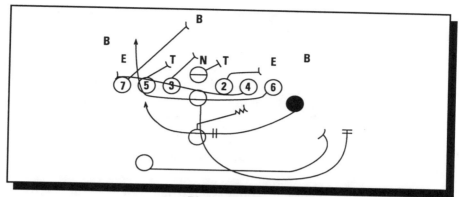

Diagram 7-24

- The Counter Criss Cross (CXX).

  The CXX is a double handoff that is designed to influence the defense. If the defensive end's assignment is to check the quarterback on the sweep boot action, then his movement outside will open the counter hole.

  a.   Right 37 Counter Criss Cross vs. the 52 defense (Diagram 7-25).

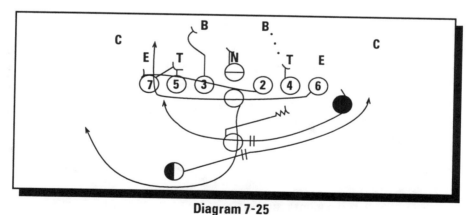

Diagram 7-25

All assignments are the same except:

    QB   Hands off to the sweep back as soon as possible
          and then fakes the sweep boot action.
    FB   Executes 30 series and plugs first unblocked color.
    HB   Controls his speed without "giving a clue."
          Receives the ball from the QB and gives the ball to
          the Wing. Then, fakes the sweep carry.
    WB   Jabs up on his outside foot and then gets on his
          counter path, comes to the HB, receives the ball
          and runs the counter hole.

It is not necessary, at this point, to diagram the counter criss cross
against all defenses, since it is the same counter blocking.

- The Counter Criss Cross Lateral Call.

Since the wingbacks have already learned to pitch the ball on the
counter lateral, it is very easy to run a counter criss cross lateral play,
which places extreme pressure on the defense if the defenders gather
to stop the counter criss cross (Diagram 7-26).

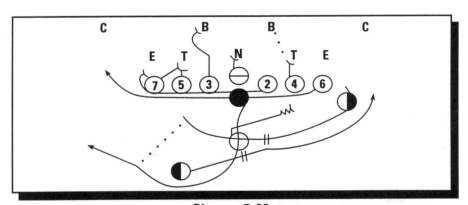

Diagram 7-26

All assignments remain the same as in counter lateral except:

    QB   After the sweep hand off, get a lateral position for
          the pitch and hang until the ball is released.
    HB   Execute the CXX play.

CHAPTER 8

The Counter Boot Package

Properly executing all fakes and the "run first" philosophy of the quarterback are the keys that make the counter boot package effective as a third threat on the "Mis-Direction Three Points of Attack" offensive style.

Similar to other parts of the Mis-direction Wing-T offense, the formations and actions of the counter boot package must be fully mixed on all counter boot calls. In other words, counter boots must be mixed into the play selection procedure and in all situations of field width and depth, as well as in all down and yardage situations to gain positioning.

- The 20 Counter Boot

    a. Right 27 Counter Boot vs. the 52 defense (Diagram 8-1).

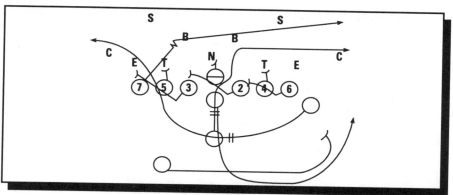

Diagram 8-1

C	Base, seal to the ball as he checks the linebacker.
PG	Trap opposite guard hole.
PT	Base, down.
PE	Influence pull and trap first color to show.
BG	Trap the defensive end.
BT	Base (in gap, on, outside).
BE	Fake the BAB, release to daylight across the field.

QB	Sell the fullback trap, sell the counter, then boot the ball wide. Attack the line of scrimmage and run. The QB has the option of throwing, if a receiver is open and if the QB feels he can get the ball to him.
FB	Sell the trap for five yards, then sprint to the sideline.
HB	Get wall position on first color to show.
CX Back	Sell the counter fully; check the throwback coverage.

b. Left Fly 27 Counter Boot vs. the 43 defense (Diagram 8-2).

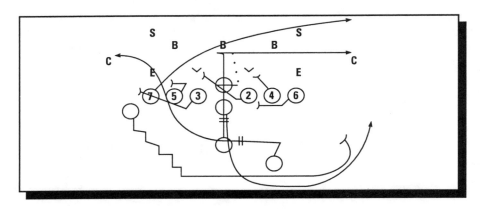

Diagram 8-2

c. Right Double 27 Counter Boot vs. the Split defense (Diagram 8-3).

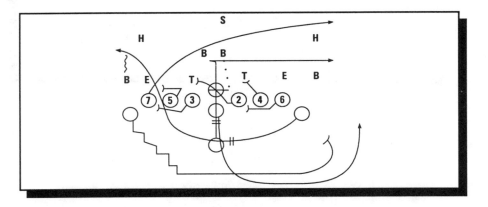

Diagram 8-3

d. Right 27 Counter Boot vs. the Eagle defense (Diagram 8-4).

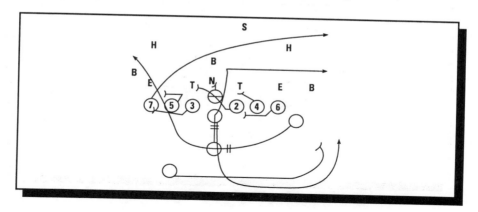

Diagram 8-4

- The 30 Series Counter Boot Call.

    This call gives us more receivers but less faking. It is usually effective due to the flooding of the three receivers and the throwback possibility.

a. Right 37 Counter Boot vs. the 52 defense (Diagram 8-5).

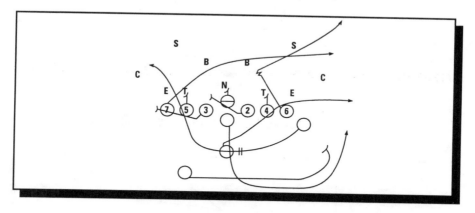

Diagram 8-5

    All assignments are the same as the 20 series except:

PE   Fake the BAB and break the flag angle.
BE   Fake BAB and cross at 15.
FB   Step up on opposite foot, then find a way to get into the flat no deeper than five yards.
QB   The same as for 20 series and reminder of "run first" philosophy.

b. Left Fly 37 Counter Boot vs. the 43 defense (Diagram 8-6).

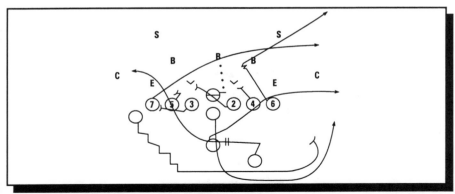

Diagram 8-6

c. Right Double 37 Counter Boot vs. the Split defense (Diagram 8-7).

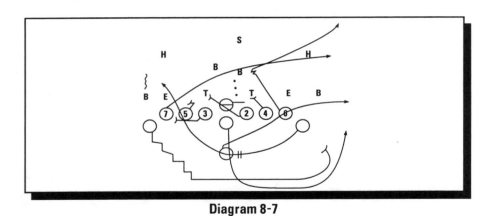

Diagram 8-7

d. Right 37 Counter Boot vs. the Eagle defense (Diagram 8-8).

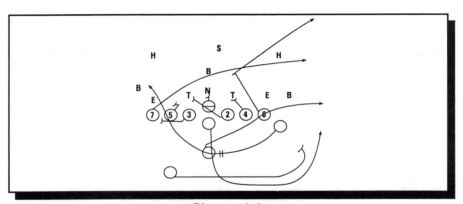

Diagram 8-8

- The 37 Counter Boot Throwback Call.

The coaches in the press box must note the defensive reaction to the counter back during the running of the counter boot. If the defense is not covering the counter back or if it is not covering him in certain areas, then we want to execute the counter boot throwback because the counterback is wide open.

a. Right 37 Counter Boot Throwback (Diagram 8-9).

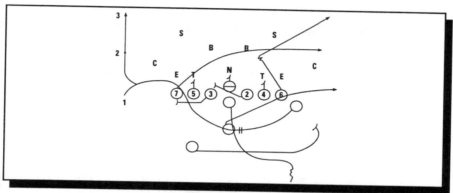

Diagram 8-9

All assignments are the same as for 37 counter boot except:

Counter Back   Fake the counter but make a "poor" one to show the defenders that he definitely does not have the ball. Get into the position for the throwback as called.

   √ If a 1 pattern is called, get on the line of scrimmage 10 yards wide and face the QB.
   √ If a 2 pattern is called, turn upfield after 10 yards and hang at 7 to 10 yards.
   √ If a 3 pattern is called, run a 2 pattern but fly deep.

QB   Check the flood receivers and "pump" the ball, then hit the throwback man as called.

b.   Left Fly 37 Counter Boot Throwback (Diagram 8-10).

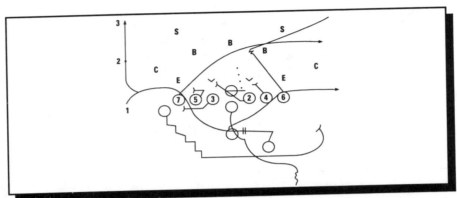

Diagram 8-10

c.   Right Double 37 Counter Boot Throwback (Diagram 8-11).

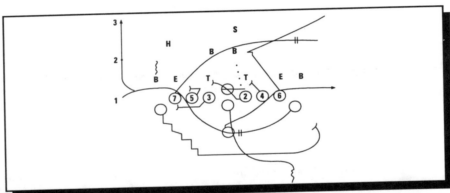

Diagram 8-11

CHAPTER 9

The Sweep Package

The "Sweep Break" as discussed in Chapter 2 is designed to carry out our "three points of attack philosophy" by presenting the sweep, the fullback trap and the sweep boot at each snap. These three plays should be called as equally as possible during the game in order to influence the pursuit of the defense.

The mixture of the three formations to each side—the right and left formations, the left and right fly formations and the right and left double formations—should be employed equally. In addition, the sweeps and the sweep boots should be run to both the wide side of the field and the short side of the field.

The backs not getting the ball must carry out "super" fakes, fully up the field. The fullback must "hide" the ball as long as possible. The quarterback must be skilled on the fake and the carry. The sweep back must cover the ball as he shifts it to his carrying pocket and he must employ super faking when he's not carrying the ball.

- The 20 Series Sweep (28 and 29)

    a. Right 28 Sweep vs. the 52 Defense (Diagram 9-1).

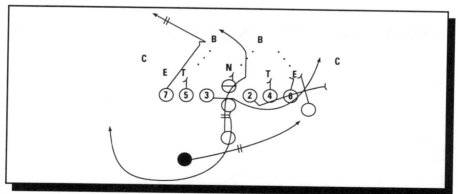

Diagram 9-1

PE	Combo block the defensive end along with the wing.
WB	Combo block the man on the tight end. Apply the BAB rule if this man aligns inside on the tight end.
PT	Base, down.
PG	Trap or log the first man outside of the wing.
C	Seal, base.
BG	Escort through hole. Read PG's hat for trap/log.
BT	Seal, base.
BE	Fake BAB, break to flag, "asking" for the pass.
QB	Sell the trap, give the ball to the sweep back, fake the sweep boot fully.
FB	Sell the trap. Plug into any threat and get upfield.
Sweepback	Come to QB slightly, get the ball and read PG's hat for the cut.

b. Left Fly 28 Sweep vs. the 43 defense (Diagram 9-2).

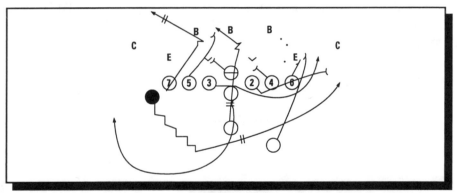

Diagram 9-2

c. Right Double 28 Sweep vs. the Split defense (Diagram 9-3).

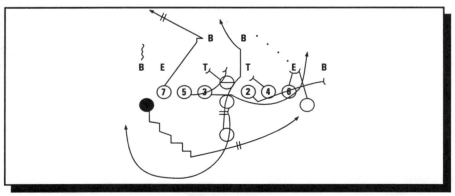

Diagram 9-3

d.   Right 28 Sweep vs. the Eagle defense (Diagram 9-4).

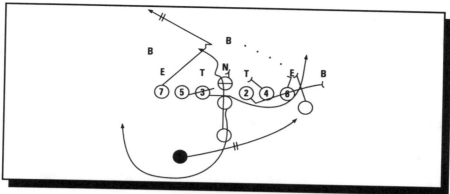

Diagram 9-4

Coaching Point: The tight end and the wingback perform a combo
block. The tight end and wing are to drive the man,
who aligns on the tight end, up the field while
reading the first inside linebacker. If the linebacker
comes to the inside, then the tight end will come
off on him. If the linebacker moves outside, then
the wing will pick him up.

√   vs. 52 (Diagram 9-5).

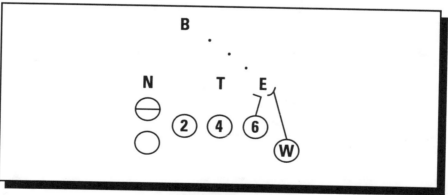

Diagram 9-5

√   vs. 43 (Diagram 9-6).

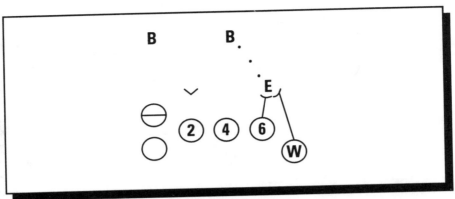

Diagram 9-6

√   vs. Split (Diagram 9-7).

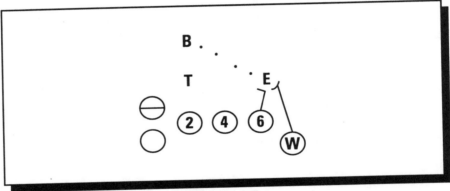

Diagram 9-7

√   vs. Eagle (Diagram 9-8).

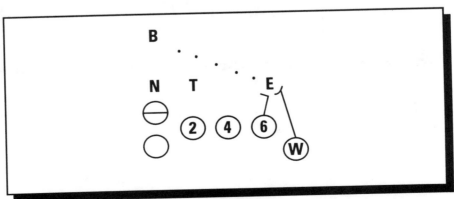

Diagram 9-8

e. vs. 8-man front defensive end who aligns to take inside leverage. The wing applies his BAB rule (Diagram 9-9).

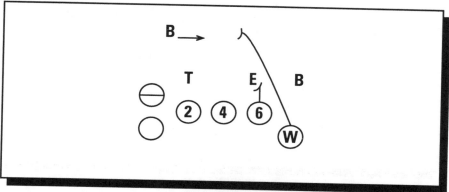

Diagram 9-9

- The 30 Series Sweep Call.

This call means that the play guard will have a base block and the fullback will become the trap/log man. Although we lose the fake to the fullback on the sweep, we gain a base blocker to the playside in case we are getting pressure through the playside guard's pull hole. All other assignments remain the same except for the play guard and the fullback. In addition, the center's rule changes since the play guard is not pulling.

a. Right 38 Sweep vs. the 52 defense (Diagram 9-10).

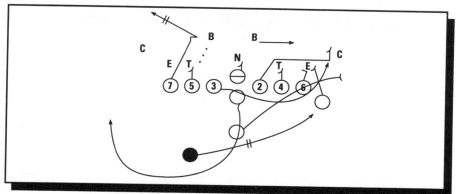

Diagram 9-10

PG   Base, fold.
C   Base, away (since PG is base, the center does not need to seal first).
FB   Kick or log the first to show outside of the wing's block.

b. Left Fly 38 Sweep vs. the 43 defense (Diagram 9-11).

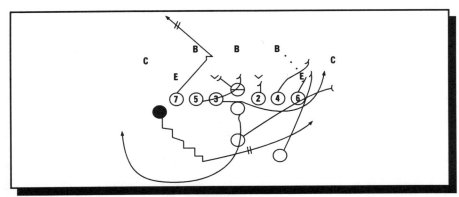

Diagram 9-11

c. Right Double 38 Sweep vs. the Split defense (Diagram 9-12).

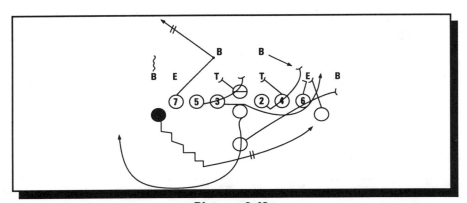

Diagram 9-12

Coaching Point: Play guard and play tackle must call a switch if the play guard cannot base his man.

d. Right 38 Sweep vs. the Eagle defense (Diagram 9-13).

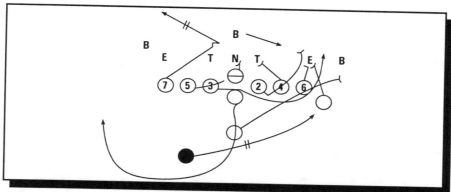

Diagram 9-13

Coaching Point: The play guard and the play tackle must call for a switch in assignments if the PG cannot base his man.

• The 50 Series Sweep Call

The 50 is a combination of the 20 and 30 series. Both the guards and the fullback will pull to the sweep. All assignments remain the same as the 20 series, except for the fullback who will escort through the hole reading the hat of the play guard for the cut. In reality, the back guard and the fullback will enter the hole shoulder to shoulder.

a. Right 58 Sweep vs. the 52 defense (Diagram 9-14).

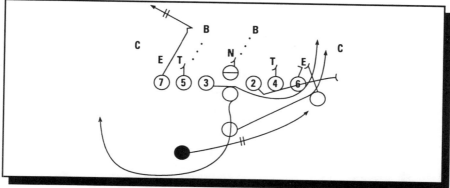

Diagram 9-14

b. Left Fly 58 Sweep vs. the 43 defense (Diagram 9-15).

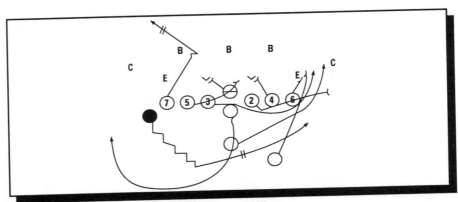

Diagram 9-15

c. Right Double 58 Sweep vs. the Split defense (Diagram 9-16).

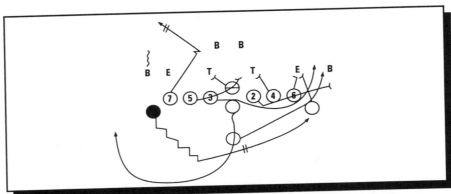

Diagram 9-16

d. Right 58 Sweep vs. the Eagle defense (Diagram 9-17).

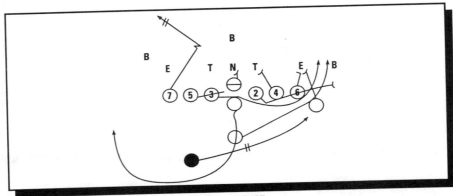

Diagram 9-17

- The 40 Series Sweep Call

This series sweep call means that the fullback will carry the ball on the sweeps. The 40 series assignments on the sweeps are the same as the 20 series. The backfield break is different.

a. Right 48 Sweep vs. the 52 defense (Diagram 9-18).

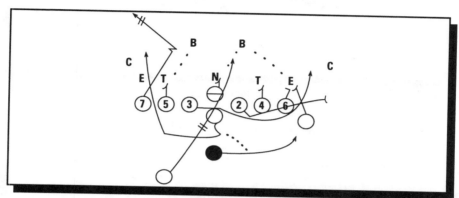

Diagram 9-18

New assignments are:

FB   Get a slight belly path. Receive the pitch and cut on play guard's hat.

HB   Slant through the outside foot of the center. Take a fake from the quarterback and sell the trap.

QB   Reverse pivot and pitch the ball to the fullback. Turn to the HB slant and sell the trap; then sell the counter carry.

Coaching Point: The 40 series break also carries out our "three points of attack" on each snap.

b. Left Fly 48 Sweep vs. the 43 defense (Diagram 9-19).

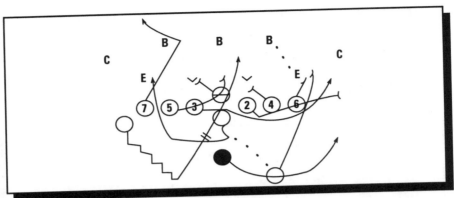

Diagram 9-19

c. Right Double 48 Sweep vs. the Split defense (Diagram 9-20).

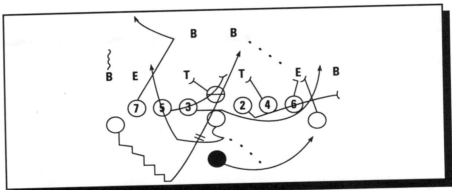

Diagram 9-20

d. Right 48 Sweep vs. the Eagle defense (Diagram 9-21).

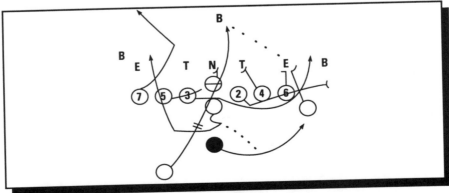

Diagram 9-21

- Two supplemental plays that complement the 40 series sweep

Play #1: The 42 Tom Trap (tackle trap).

    a.   Right 42 Tom Trap vs 52 Defense (Diagram 9-22).

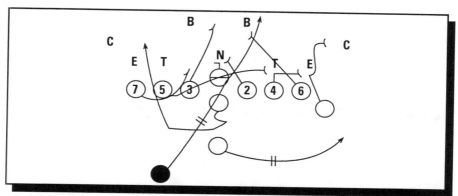

Diagram 9-22

PG	Lead, influence.
C	Post, base.
PT	Influence downman on, BAB.
PE	BAB.
BG	Base.
BT	Trap first downman past center.
BE	Seal PT hole.
WB	Fake lead and wall contain.
FB	Fake the sweep.
QB	Fake the pitch, turn and give ball to HB, then fake your counter.
HB	Slant at out foot of center, take ball and cut on the BAB block.

b. Left Fly 42 Tom Trap vs. the 43 defense (Diagram 9-23).

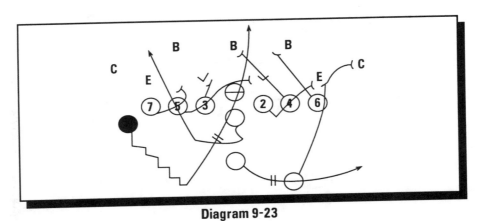

Diagram 9-23

c. Right Double 42 Tom Trap vs. the Split defense (Diagram 9-24).

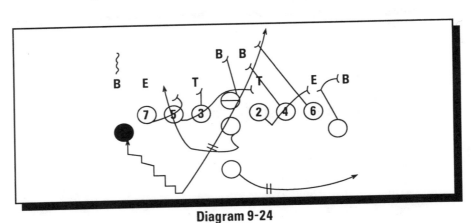

Diagram 9-24

d. Right 24 Tom Trap vs. the Eagle defense (Diagram 9-25).

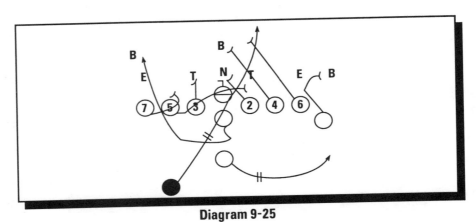

Diagram 9-25

Play #2: The 47 QB Counter Down.

a. Right 47 QB Counter Down vs. the 52 defense (Diagram 9-26).

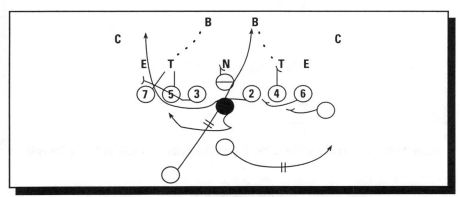

Diagram 9-26

PE   Down, combo.
PT   Down, combo.
PG   Trap/log first outside of PE's down.
C   Base, away.
BG   Escort.
BT   Seal, base.
BE   Seal, base.
W   Seal, base.
FB   Fake your sweep.
HB   Sell the trap.
QB   Fake the pitch, sell the trap, tuck the ball and read PG's hat for the cut.

b. Left Fly 47 QB Counter Down vs. the 43 defense (Diagram 9-27).

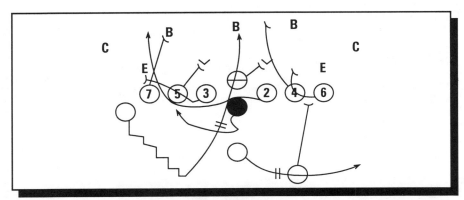

Diagram 9-27

c. Right Double 47 QB Counter Down vs. the Split defense (Diagram 9-28).

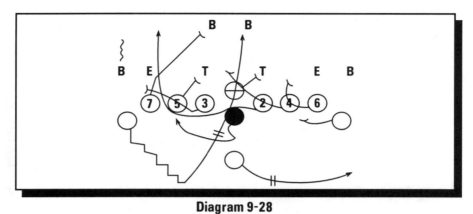

Diagram 9-28

d. Right 47 QB Counter Down vs. the Eagle defense (Diagram 9-29).

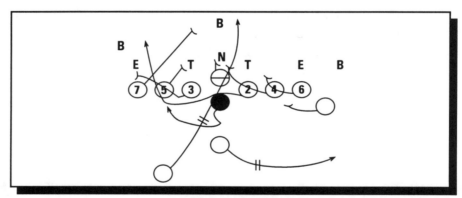

Diagram 9-29

- The down blocking scheme on sweep plays

  a. Right 28 Sweep vs. the 52 defense (Diagram 9-30).

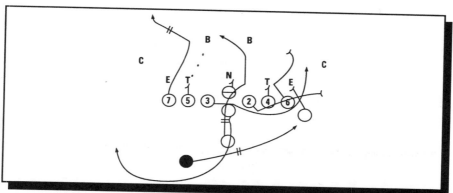

Diagram 9-30

All assignments are the same as in the power blocking scheme except:

Wing/HB	Down on man on tight end, combo.
PE	Down, combo.
PT	Down, combo.
C	Base, away.

  b. Left Fly 28 Sweep Down vs. the 43 defense (Diagram 9-31).

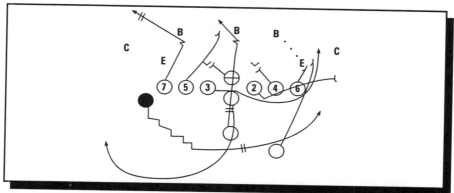

Diagram 9-31

c.   Right Double 28 Sweep Down vs. the Split defense (Diagram 9-32).

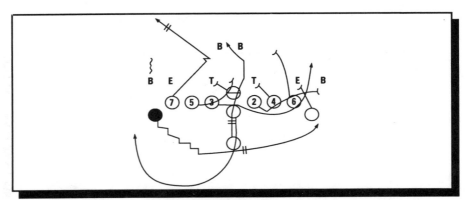

Diagram 9-32

d.   Right 28 Sweep Down vs. the Eagle defense (Diagram 9-33).

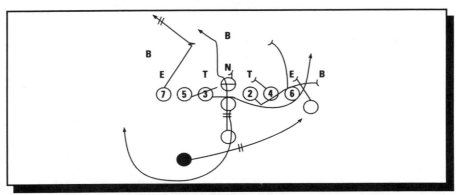

Diagram 9-33

7.   The base blocking scheme for sweep plays.

The base scheme on sweep plays means that we are actually going to attempt to out-distance the defense wide. By stretching the defense, we will either be successful in getting wide or we will get a cut up or a cut back while the defenders are in a stretched situation.

a. Right 28 Sweep Base vs. the 52 defense (Diagram 9-34).

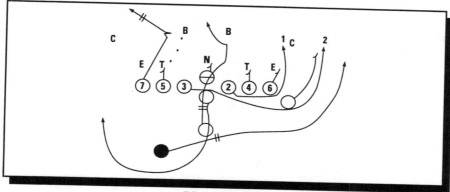

Diagram 9-34

WB/HB	Base-reach block #4 or contain man.
PE	Base.
PT	Base, down.
PG	Pull alley #1, which is three yards outside of the PE's block. The PG will secure his block first.
C	Seal, base.
BG	Pull alley #2, which is three yards outside of wing/halfback's reach block. This block will be secured first.
BT	Seal, base.
BE	Usual when backside from sweeps.

All other backs remain the same in relation to the series called.

b. Left Fly 28 Sweep Base vs. the 43 defense (Diagram 9-35).

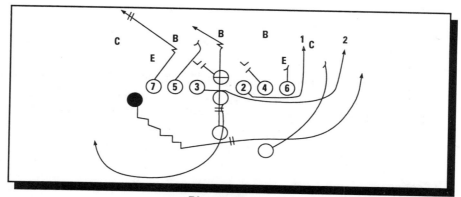

Diagram 9-35

c. Right Double 28 Sweep Base vs. the Split defense (Diagram 9-36).

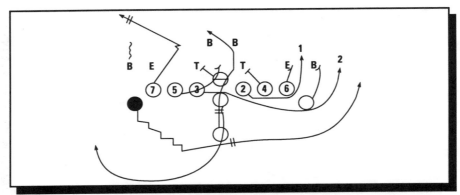

Diagram 9-36

d. Right 28 Sweep Base vs. the Eagle defense (Diagram 9-37).

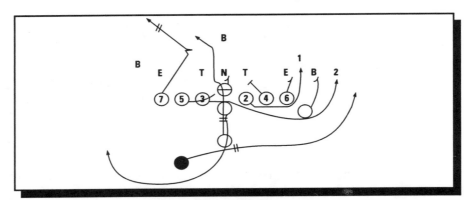

Diagram 9-37

• The "Switch" Call added to the sweep play.

The switch call when added to the sweep means that the wing and the tight end to the side of the sweep will switch assignments—the wing will block down and the tight end will pull around and reach block the contain man. This "switch" call has proven very effective as a surprise to the defenders. We prefer to call the "switch" off the double formation because we get a "jump" on the defense with the momentum of the fly back. The defense cannot key the fly since we fly and counter and use the sweep boot back behind the fly action. We also like the "switch" call from the 50 series.

a. Right 58 Sweep Base Switch vs. the 52 defense (Diagram 9-38).

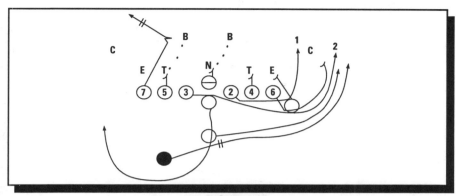

Diagram 9-38

All assignments remain the same as the base call, except for the wing and the tight end.

b. Right Double 58 Sweep Base Switch vs. the 43 defense (Diagram 9-39).

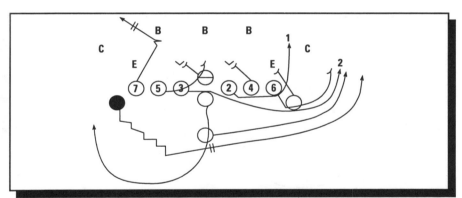

Diagram 9-39

c. Right Double 58 Sweep Base Switch vs. the Split defense (Diagram 9-40). Many 8-man front defenses do not commit their contain man to the line of scrimmage until the key is read.

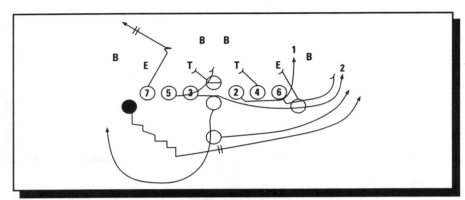

Diagram 9-40

d. Right 58 Sweep Base Switch vs. the Eagle defense (Diagram 9-41). Many 8-man front defenses do not commit their contain man to the line of scrimmage until the keys are read.

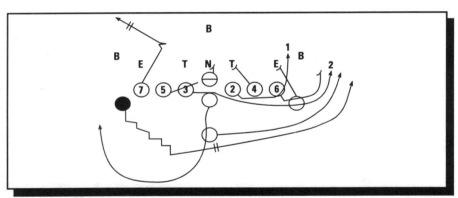

Diagram 9-41

e. Right Double 58 Sweep Base Switch vs. the 52 defense (Diagram 9-42).

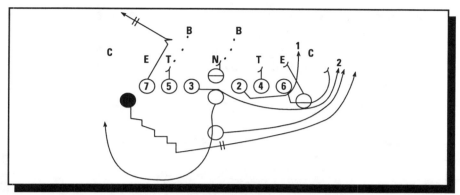

Diagram 9-42

• The toss sweep

We also run the "Toss Sweep" which is being employed in wholesale fashion by many teams across the country, because everyone wants to get the extra blocker in the person of the quarterback. Since we already employ the word "toss" in our fullback trap toss to the tight end, we use the word, "pitch" added to our sweep plays when we want the quarterback to lead the play. We add the word "pitch" to any of our sweeps and to all of the series and all of the formations. The double formation with the fly back has worked well with the pitch for us. Diagram 9-43 illustrates the pitch sweep out of the left fly formation—a play which has been successful for us since the defense does not usually expect a sweep into the tight end-halfback side of the formation.

a. Left Fly 58 Sweep Base Pitch vs. the 52 defense (Diagram 9-43).

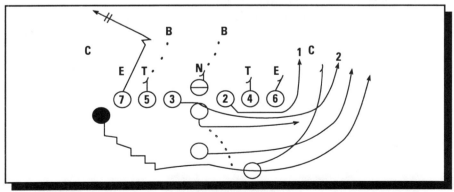

Diagram 9-43

- The Inside Sweep (26 and 27)

We have been in games where the defense assumes an alignment as if to say "you are not going to run the sweep tonight." Even though some of these defenses, by aligning to stop the sweep, loosened and allowed the counter, we were fortunate to have capability to run the inside sweep.

a. Right 26 Sweep Down vs. the 52 defense (Diagram 9-44).

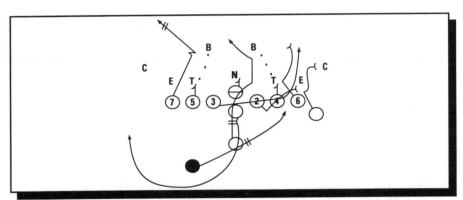

Diagram 9-44

PE	Down, combo, BAB.
PT	Down, combo.
PG	Trap first downman past the PT.
C	Base, away.
BG	Escort.
BT	Seal, base.
BE	Usual assignment on sweeps away.
FB	Sell the trap through the linebacker.
Wing	Suba (set up the DE and block away).
HB	Slant through the FB's heels, take the ball, cut the hole.
QB	Sell the trap. Do not force the HB deep. Give on the sweep, sell the boot.

b. Left Fly 26 Sweep Down vs. 43 defense (Diagram 9-45).

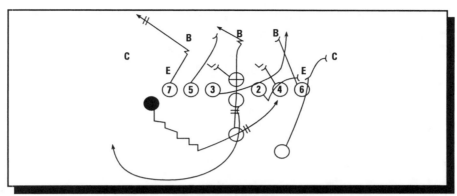

Diagram 9-45

c. Right Double 26 Sweep Down vs. the Split defense (Diagram 9-46).

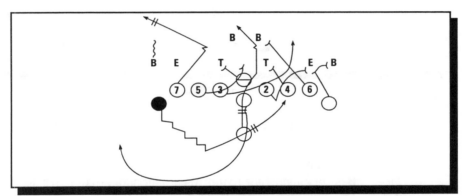

Diagram 9-46

d. Right 26 Sweep Down vs. the Eagle defense (Diagram 9-47).

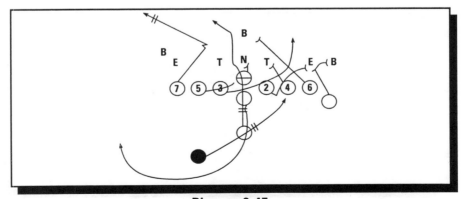

Diagram 9-47

- The Inside Sweep off the 30 series (36 and 37)

If the fullback is an effective blocker, we mix the inside sweep on both the 20 and the 30 series. Sometimes, the 30 sweep is more effective since we get to double up on the first downman on or inside of the play tackle, thereby creating a bigger hole; But we lose the trap fake. We really like the trap fake whenever possible.

a. Right 36 Sweep vs. the 52 defense (Diagram 9-48).

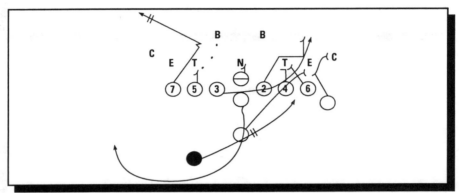

Diagram 9-48

Essentially, all assignments are the same as the 20 series except:

PG   Base, post.
FB   It is very important to get the proper angle to get an inside-out blocking angle and kick out the first downman outside the PT.

b. Left Fly 36 Sweep vs. the 43 defense (Diagram 9-49).

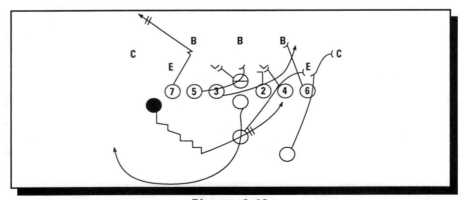

Diagram 9-49

c. Right Double 36 Sweep vs. the Split defense (Diagram 9-50).

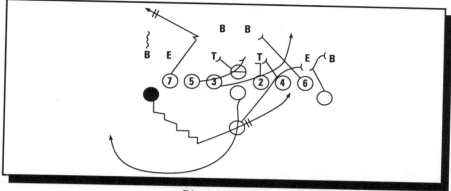

Diagram 9-50

d. Right 36 Sweep vs. the Eagle defense (Diagram 9-51).

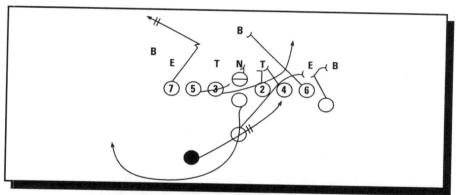

Diagram 9-51

- Quarterback counter play off the 20 series

A quarterback counter play off the 20 series inside sweep has been very effective for us. The blocking is the same as for the 47 QB counter from the 40 series as detailed earlier. It is important that the quarterback stay low in order to keep from exposing himself too early to the defense.

a. Right 17 QB Counter Down vs. the 52 defense (Diagram 9-52).

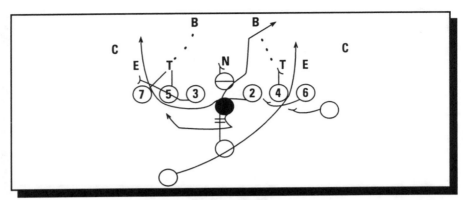

Diagram 9-52

PE	Down, combo.
PT	Down, combo.
PG	Trap/log first outside of PE's down.
C	Base, away.
BG	Escort.
BT	Seal, base.
BE	Seal, base.
WB/HB	Seal.
FB	Sell the trap.
HB	Lift your inside arm as you go past the QB; fake your inside sweep.
QB	Sell the trap, step back and tuck the ball as the HB comes by. Stay low and read the hat of the trap/log.

b. Left Fly 17 QB Counter Down vs. the 43 defense (Diagram 9-53).

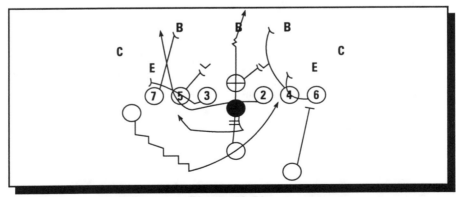

Diagram 9-53

c. Right Double 17 QB Counter Down vs. the Split defense (Diagram 9-54).

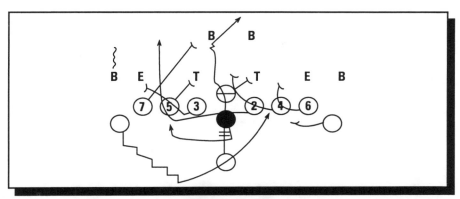

Diagram 9-54

d. Right 17 QB Counter Down vs. the Eagle defense (Diagram 9-55).

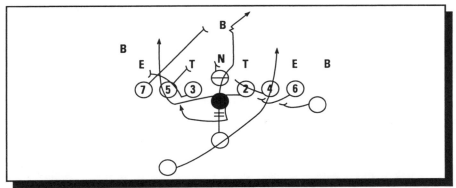

Diagram 9-55

CHAPTER 10

The Sweep Boot Package

The Sweep Boot Package is the third leg of our "three points of attack" off of the sweep break. The fakes by the backs in selling the fullback trap and in selling the sweep, along with the philosophy that the quarterback must come out with "run intent" and attack the defense, are the keys to a successful bootleg package. If the quarterback uses all of his speed from the snap and gets outside of the defense, he has the option of either the run or the pass. Not surprisingly, this aspect really puts pressure on the defense.

We find that a very high percentage of the bootleg plays result in big yardage gains or in touchdowns. The bootlegs are also very good calls in short yardage and goal line situations, if the "run first intent" is accomplished. Any time the quarterback gets outside with both the run and the pass options open, very good things can happen.

- The 20 Series Sweep Boot (28 and 29)

    a. Right 28 Sweep Boot vs. the 52 defense (Diagram 10-1).

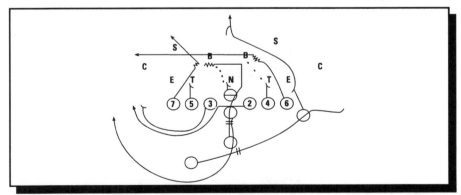

Diagram 10-1

PE   Sell the BAB and break the flag angle.
PT   Base down.
PG   Serve as the wall guard. Pull deep (three yards deep from behind the heels of the PTE). Eyes in on the first unblocked opponent. Get a wall-in position and prevent him from moving outside.
C   Seal, base, away.

BG   Serve as the escort guard. Pull as in the trap; track the wall guard. Get a depth of four yards from the PTE's heels. Wall in any color coming to the quarterback. Both guards must "spring" the QB outside.

BT   Seal, base, hinge.

BE   Sell the BAB, cut across at a basic 10-12 yards deep. Find a "hole" between 6 and 15 yards deep. Hang when open; run when covered.

FB   Sell the trap up to five yards. Plug anyone coming to the quarterback. Slide to the ball side, but do not pass the PTE position. Then, stop and become a safety valve receiver.

WB   Hit the DE hard, then get an angle at the middle of the goal posts. Do not cross the original position of the football. Fly deep, but if covered, execute a comeback to 15 yards.

HB   Sell the sweep until his feet are on the line of scrimmage, then widen and "die off" while observing the defensive coverage for a throwback call.

QB   Sell the trap. Sell the sweep. Hide the ball from the ball side of the defense. Use all his speed from the snap. Do not "hang;" attack the defense all the way. Get outside of all opponents and take the run. If an open receiver is spotted, throw the ball on the run. If no one is open, take the run. At the point that the QB knows he is running, he should yell "GO" to his guards so that they may cross the line of scrimmage.

Coaching Points:

√   The guards must not cross the line of scrimmage unless they hear "GO" by the quarterback.

√   The quarterback may still throw even if he has made the go call, if he notes that the guards have not crossed.

√   Half of the bootlegs should be called off the fly action. In addition, half of the bootlegs should be made into the short side of the field.

√   The fakes and the quarterback mechanics are the keys to a successful bootleg attack.

b. Left Fly 28 Sweep Boot vs. the 43 defense (Diagram 10-2).

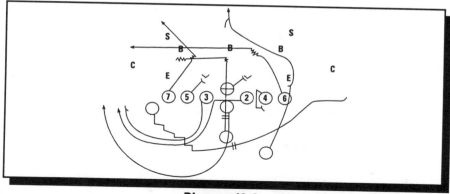

Diagram 10-2

c. Right Double 28 Sweep Boot vs. the Split defense (Diagram 10-3).

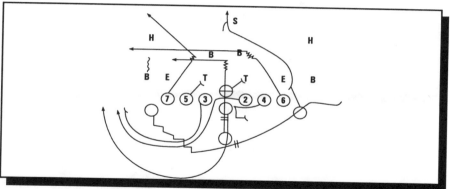

Diagram 10-3

d. Right 28 Sweep Boot vs. the Eagle defense (Diagram 10-4).

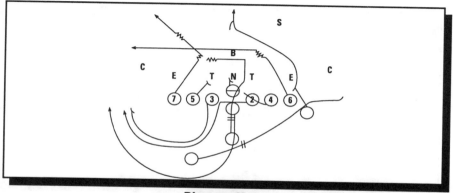

Diagram 10-4

- Change up calls for Sweep Boot Patterns.

  All assignments remain the same except for the receiver changes.

  a. 28 Sweep Boot "Switch" (Diagram 10-5).

  √ The Tight Ends will switch assignments from basic patterns.
  √ PE will fake the BAB and cork-screw into the sideline to daylight depth.
  √ BE will fake the BAB and run the flag.

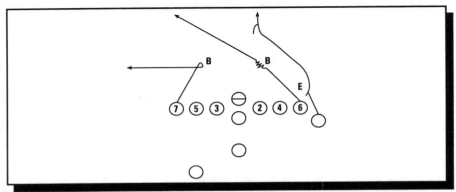

Diagram 10-5

  b. 28 Sweep Boot "Quick-Drag" (Diagram 10-6).

  √ PE will release inside and sprint to the sideline, no deeper than two yards.
  √ BE will run the flag.
  √ Wing will drag across to daylight.

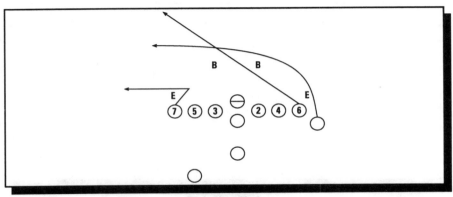

Diagram 10-6

Coaching points for sweep boot pattern strategy:

√   If the defense is covering the flat with the contain man, then call
    the basic pattern as the defensive end and inside linebacker will be
    assigned to contain the quarterback. In this case, the guards should
    be able to propel the quarterback outside in a run situation. As a
    result, the contain man is placed in a "hot box;" he has to either
    drop the receiver or allow the run.

√   If the defense is bringing the contain man to the quarterback, the
    "quick-drag" pattern should be called. In this instance, the PE will
    "out run" the coverage of the inside linebacker and become open. If
    the linebacker is fortunate to be able to cover the PE to the
    sideline, then the drag man has an excellent chance to spring open.

•   The 28 Sweep Boot "Throwback" (Diagram 10-7)

    If the defense does not assign someone to cover the sweep back,
    then get on the "throwback" right now.

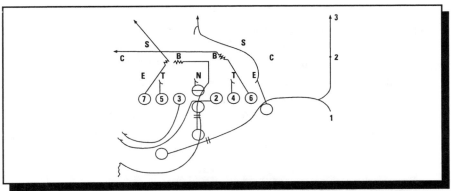

Diagram 10-7

All assignments remain the same except:

√   *The guards* will build a passing "pocket" three yards
    outside of the tight end.
√   *The quarterback* will set up in the pocket and drop off
    pumping to the receivers as he checks the throwback area.
√   *The halfback* will run the sweep to the line of scrimmage.
    Then, he will sprint out to the sideline to a point 10 yards
    wide and run the pattern as called:

1 call—face the quarterback on the line.
2 call—turn upfield and hang between 7 and 10 yards.
3 call—fly deep.

- 28 Sweep GOB (Diagram 10-8)

GOB means that the guards pull opposite the ball. This play involves a naked bootleg.

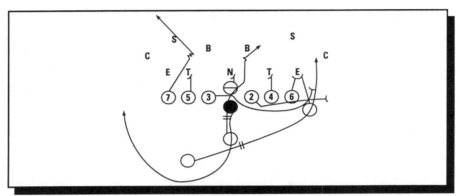

Diagram 10-8

The entire team will execute the sweep play, but no one will cross the line of scrimmage to block. The naked boot could result in a pass. The quarterback must sell the trap, sell the sweep and hide the ball. He must come out with run-first intent. The backside tight end will run the flag pattern as he does on all sweeps away from his side. The success of this play depends entirely upon the skill of the quarterback. This play is a very important one to our offense since it is a "key break" to the defense.

- The Sweep Keep (28 and 29)

When we call "boot," the ball will be going away from the flow of the play. The word, "keep," means that the ball will be kept to the flow of the play. Both boots and keeps are run/pass plays with "run intent" first. The keep play is very important to us since we must show the defense that we do throw the ball with the flow of the play. We mix the sweep keep with the sweep boot liberally.

a. Right 28 Sweep Keep vs. the 52 defense (Diagram 10-9).

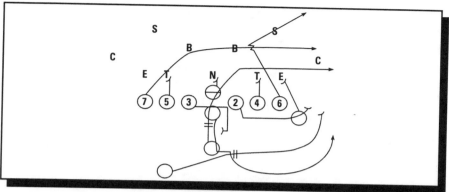

Diagram 10-9

PE   Fake BAB and flag.

PT   Base, down.

PG   Pull and check alley 1, then alley 2. Do not cross the line of scrimmage unless the quarterback yells "GO." The PG must block base if he and the PT are both covered by downmen.

C   Base, away.

BG   Pull and check the 2 hole. If no one comes through 2 hole, then hinge back for the chase man. If the PG and the center are both covered by downmen, the PG must block base.

BT   Base, in gap, hinge.

BE   Fake BAB and cross at 15 yards deep.

WB   Block down on the defensive end.

FB   Sell the trap and then get into the flat at three yards deep.

HB   Sell the sweep as long as possible, then lock-up block on the first color to show.

QB   Sell the trap, sell the sweep. Get a short ride on the sweep back, then come off with "run first intent," looking for an open receiver. The QB should yell "GO" if he decides to run.

b. Left Fly 28 Sweep Keep vs. the 43 defense (Diagram 10-10).

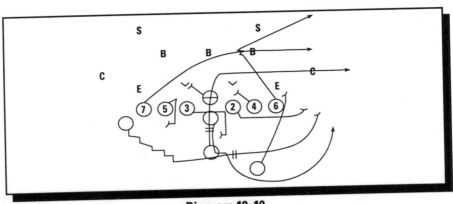

Diagram 10-10

c. Right Double 28 Sweep Keep vs. the Split defense (Diagram 10-11).

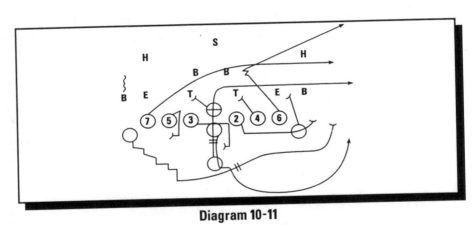

Diagram 10-11

d. Right 28 Sweep Keep vs. the Eagle defense (Diagram 10-12).

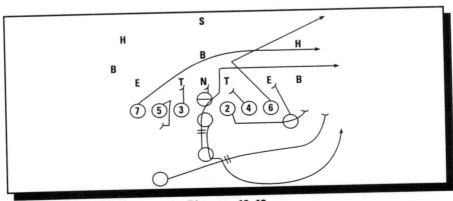

Diagram 10-12

CHAPTER 11

The Option Package

I firmly believe that all offensive systems should be able to run some type of an option in order to force the defense to align to stop it. Since the option is not basic to our offensive scheme, we try to keep it as simple as possible for our players.

The option is a part of our 40 series because the fullback's path differs from the 20, 30 and 50 series.

- The 44 Slant (45 to the left)

    a. Right 44 Slant vs. the 52 defense (Diagram 11-1).

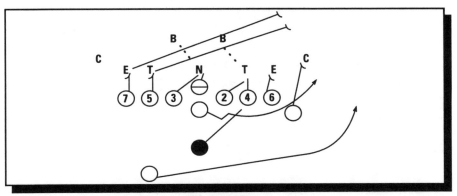

Diagram 11-1

b. Left Fly 44 Slant vs. the 43 defense (Diagram 11-2).

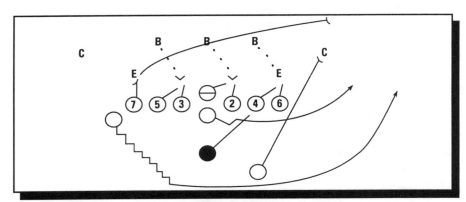

Diagram 11-2

Against 7-man front defenses, the "zone block" is preferred, although we can totally base it.

FB Slant through the butt of the PT, receive the ball, cover it with both forearms and run to daylight.

QB Get the ball to the fullback as soon as possible, and as deep as possible. Get a slight ride, then come out from behind the fullback and attack the end with speed.

HB Maintain the pitch relationship to the quarterback. The HB must hurry.

WB Base.

c. Right Double 44 Slant vs. the Split defense (Diagram 11-3).

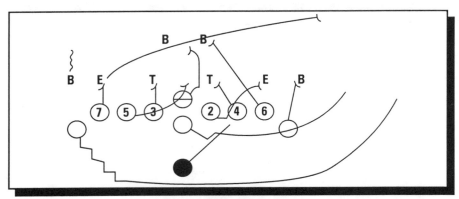

Diagram 11-3

d. Right 44 Slant vs. the Eagle defense (Diagram 11-4).

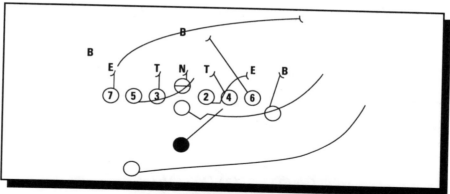

Diagram 11-4

Against 8-man front defenses which leave the PT uncovered, the G Block is preferred, even though we can base it with a fold between the PG and PT. Diagrams 11-3 and 11-4 illustrate the G Block vs. the split and the eagle defenses.

PE	Down.
PT	Down.
PG	Trap the defensive end.
C	Base, play gap, linebacker.
BG	Base.
BT	Seal, BAH (block across the hole).
BE	BAH.

- The 44 Slant-Option (45 Slant-Option to the left).

Simplicity is continued in the option game by zone blocking the option as far as feasible.

a. Right 44 Slant-Option vs. the 52 defense (Diagram 11-5).

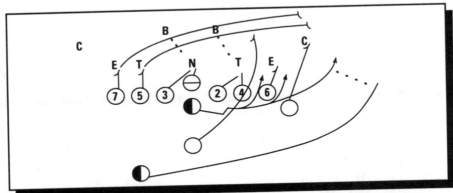

Diagram 11-5

FB   Sell the 44 Slant; but he must become a blocker for the quarterback by finding the linebacker or other unblocked opponent and drive through with his inside shoulder.

QB   Meet the fullback as in 44 Slant, but observe the defensive reaction as he "rides." His first intent should be to keep the ball. Find a hole:

√   Follow the fullback.
√   Cut outside the defensive end.
√   Keep wide.
√   His last choice should be to pitch the ball.

b. Left Fly 44 Slant-Option vs. the 43 defense (Diagram 11-6).

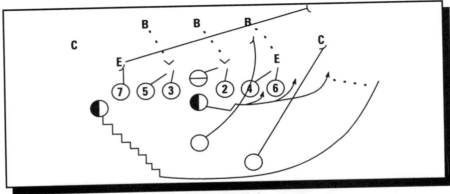

Diagram 11-6

c. Right Double 44 Slant-Option vs. the Split defense (Diagram 11-7).

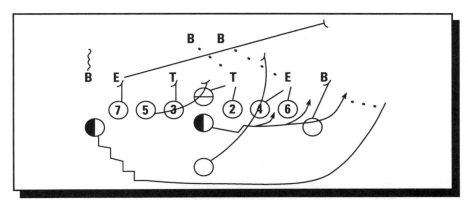

Diagram 11-7

d. Right 44 Slant-Option vs. the Eagle defense (Diagram 11-8).

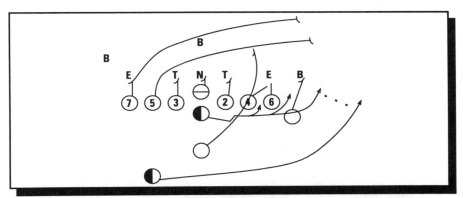

Diagram 11-8

CHAPTER 12

Wing-T Supplement

Over the years, we have supplemented the Wing-T offense with various activities. While some of these supplements have proven to be somewhat unsuccessful, a few have had a positive impact. This chapter presents a discussion of the three supplements that have proven valuable over the years:

- The double wing (without a pre-fly by a wing and snap the ball on first sound)
- The power formation
- The wing I formation

The Double Call

To reiterate, when we call "Right Double," both halfbacks will align in the wing positions. The word, "right," called before the "double," means that the left wing will fly. As a result, we are in wing right formation at the snap. The same is true for the "Left Double" call.

Early on, in the more than two decades that my teams employed this offense, I recognized the need to design something from the double formation that did not use the fly action before the snap. The purpose of the no-fly-double wing is to surprise the defense, thereby causing the defenders to first align to cover the double wing in case there is no fly, and, subsequently, to adjust if there was a pre-fly.

The double wing set did not appear to influence the 4-back (7-man front) defenses very much, except to cause the cornerbacks or contain men to align deeper until the fly occurred (Diagrams 12-1 and 12-2).

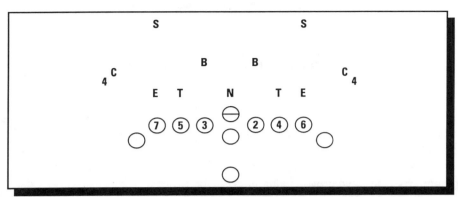

Diagram 12-1

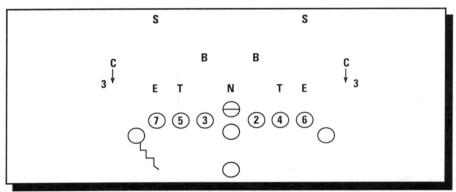

Diagram 12-2

The double wing set did influence the alignment of the 3-back (8-man front) defenses to some extent, by causing the outside linebackers to align much deeper until a pre-fly occurred. When the wing left on the pre-fly, the contain linebacker had to move to the contain position very quickly and rarely made it to the line of scrimmage before the snap. It should be remembered that the fly we use is a full speed one-count movement (Diagram 12-3).

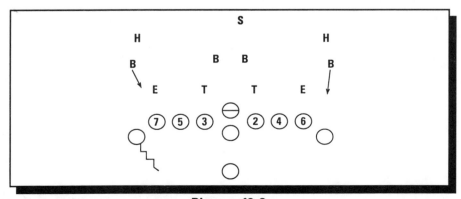

Diagram 12-3

In the double wing (no fly) formation, a "suddenly dropback pass" attack was implemented to try to take advantage of the defense.

- • "Suddenly Dropback Pass" vs. the 4-back, 7-man front type of defense.

   We have found that the vast majority of these 4-back defenses will employ cover 2 (halves) style of pass and contain coverage. The cornerbacks will align four yards deep and four yards wide, while the safeties will align 10-12 yards deep and head up on the tight ends (Diagram 12-4).

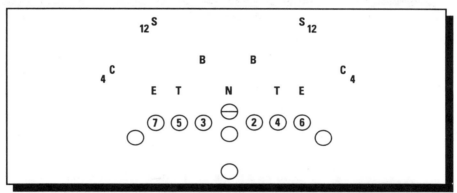

Diagram 12-4

   If the tight ends release, the safeties will cover their half of the field, while the corners will cover the flats. If the tight ends block, the corners will contain and the safeties will support.

   With these facts in mind, we designed our "suddenly dropback pass" patterns.

   a. Double Dropback Call vs. the 4-back cover 2 (Diagrams 12-5 and 12-6).

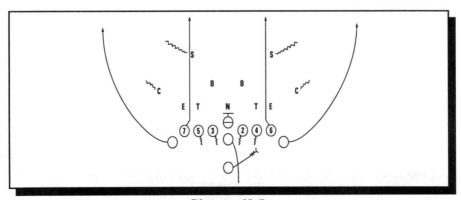

Diagram 12-5

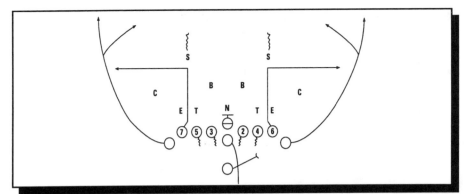

Diagram 12-6

Tight Ends   Get upfield via the best release. Run at the safety. If the safety leaves, continue deep and look for the ball inside. If the safety stays, square out and sprint to the sideline looking for the ball.

Wings   Come off at full speed. Get depth and width. Force the defense to cover the entire field. Outrun the corner coverage. If the corner does not cover him deep, the wings should look for the "fly ball" inside. If the corner mans the wing, the wing should outrun him, while looking for the fly ball. If the corner does a good job in manning the wings, the wings should cut to the post.

Quarterback   Open to the QB's right, drop seven steps, as he keys the safety's action and surveys the field. The scout report of each opponent will identify suspect personnel.

b.   Double Dropback Call vs. 3-back zone coverage (Diagram 12-7).

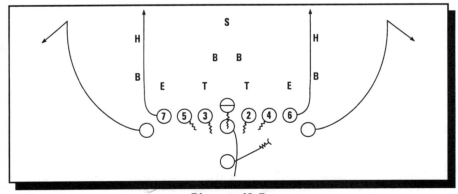

Diagram 12-7

When a single safety alignment is observed:

Tight Ends   Release wide outside (stretch the middle zone). Sprint deep looking inside for the ball.

Wings   Basic wide-deep release. The wings will draw halfback coverage either man or zone. The wings should entertain the halfback by making the HB stretch to him and then execute a sideline comeback. If the wings get the outside linebacker on man-to-man coverage, they should beat them deep.

Quarterback   Same as described for 4-back coverage.

Coaching Point: If outside linebacker coverage on the wings is drawn, we will add "B Swing" to the call, (B is the fullback) as shown in Diagram 12-8.

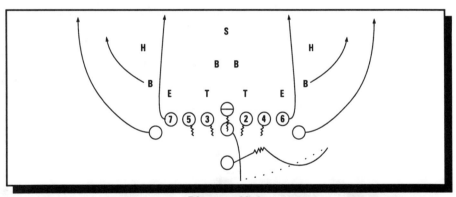

Diagram 12-8

c.   Pass protection for the Double Dropback Call.

   √   vs. 52 (Diagram 12-9).

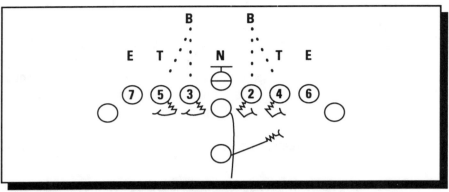

Diagram 12-9

   √   vs. 43 (Diagram 12-10).

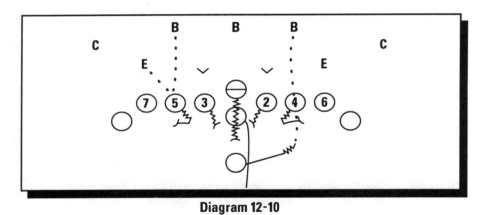

Diagram 12-10

√   vs. Split (Diagram 12-11).

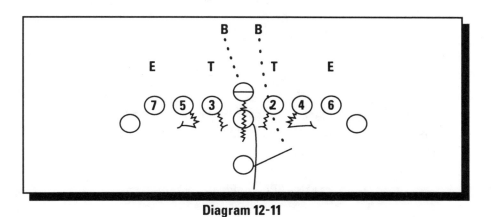

Diagram 12-11

√   vs. the Eagle (Diagram 12-12).

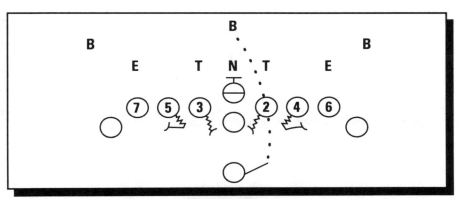

Diagram 12-12

Bear in mind that this action is a sudden surprise for the defense which must purely react to the play without focus time. Accordingly, we snap the ball on the first sound.

The front 5 will drop back quickly at the snap, reading the man coming to their zone. This situation involves a "cup-number" scheme.

C	zero zone.
G's	1 zone.
T's	2 zone.
FB	block #3 to right.

Coaching Point: If the defense comes with seven rushers, the weak
defensive end would be free. The problem for the
defense is that they have to predict when this play
will come.

- The Power Set (a supplement to the Wing-T)

In this set, the halfback aligns over to the side of the wing. All other
positions remain the same. Our huddle call is "power right" and "power left"
(Diagrams 12-13 and 12-14).

Power Right

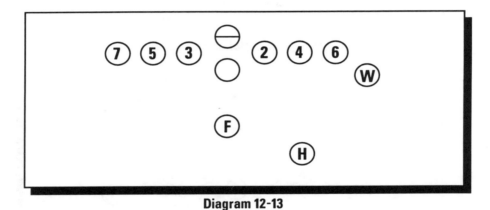

Diagram 12-13

Power Left

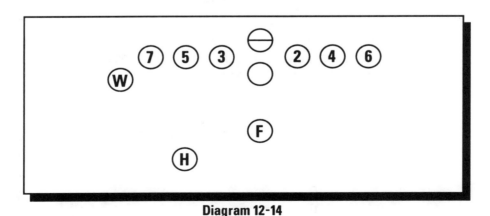

Diagram 12-14

From the power set, we are able to run the majority of our basic offense:

- The fullback package (Chapter 6);
- The counter package (Chapter 7);
- The counter boot package (Chapter 8);
- The 40 sweep to the power side;
- The 20, 30 and 50 sweeps to the weak side;
- The sweep boot package (showing weak sweep and booting back to power);
- The option package (Chapter 11).

The Power Set Breaks

The Counter Break (Diagram 12-15)

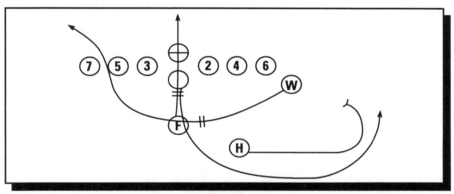

Diagram 12-15

Sweep Break—20 series strong (Diagram 12-16)

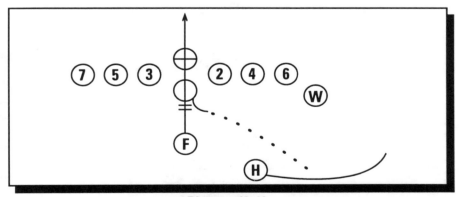

Diagram 12-16

Sweep Break—40 series (Diagram 12-17)

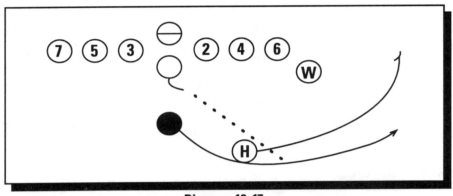

Diagram 12-17

Sweep Break—20 series weak (Diagram 12-18)

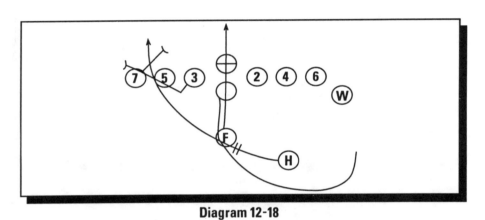

Diagram 12-18

Sweep Break—30 and 50 series weak (Diagram 12-19)

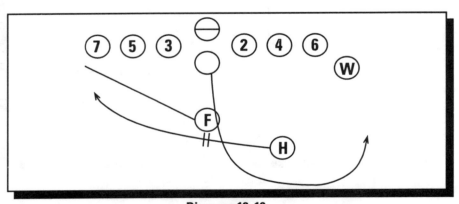

Diagram 12-19

The Strong-side Shoot Call (28 and 29 Shoot)

The play that gets advantage on the defense (if the defenders fail to adjust) is the shoot call to the strong or wing side. We will call this play early in our game plan from the power set. This step forces the defense to adjust to stop this play. We will then go to whatever the adjustment gives us—particularly, the weak side.

    a.   Power Right 28 Shoot Down vs. the 52 defense (Diagram 12-20).

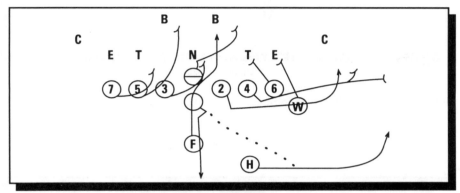

Diagram 12-20

    b.   Power Right 28 Shoot Base vs. the 43 defense (Diagram 12-21).

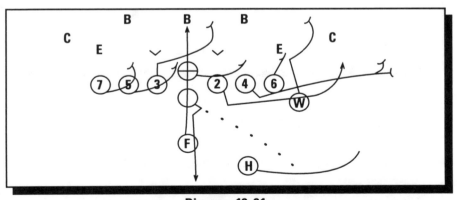

Diagram 12-21

Coaching Point: Note base call.

c. Power Right 28 Shoot Base vs. the Split defense (Diagram 12-22).

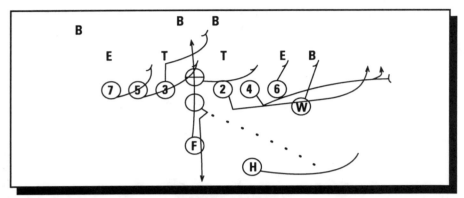

Diagram 12-22

Coaching Point: Note base call.

d. Power Right 28 Shoot vs. the Eagle defense (Diagram 12-23).

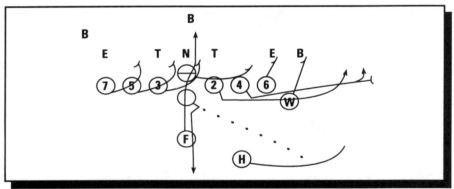

Diagram 12-23

Coaching Point: Note base call.

• The Wing I Set (as a supplement to the Wing-T)

The halfback will align over to the wing side in the tailback position. All other positions will remain the same. The huddle call is, "I Right" and "I Left" (Diagrams 12-24 and 12-25).

I Right

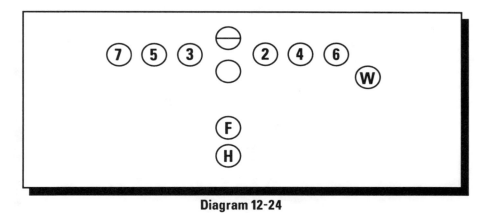

Diagram 12-24

I Left

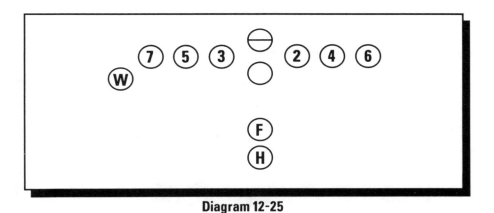

Diagram 12-25

From the I Set, we are able to run the majority of our basic offense:

The fullback package (Chapter 6);
The counter package (Chapter 7);
The counter boot package (Chapter 8);
The 20, 30 and 50 sweep package (Chapter 9);
The option package (Chapter 11).

The I Set Breaks

The Counter Break (Diagram 12-26)

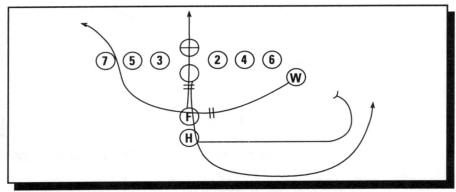

Diagram 12-26

The Sweep Break—20 series (Diagram 12-27)

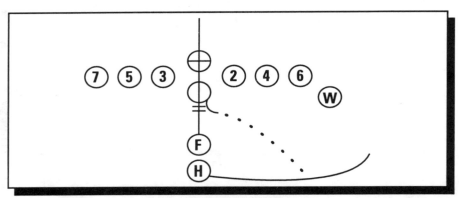

Diagram 12-27

The Sweep Break—30,50 series (Diagram 12-28)

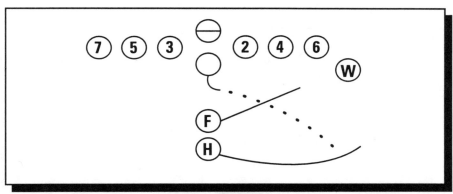

Diagram 12-28

The Strong-side 50 Sweep Call (58 and 59)

The play that we like to call out of the Wing I formation is the 50 sweep. This play jumps on the defense "in a hurry." After we see what defensive adjustments are made, other plays from the Wing I are mixed.

    a.   I Right 58 Sweep Base vs. the 52 defense (Diagram 12-29).

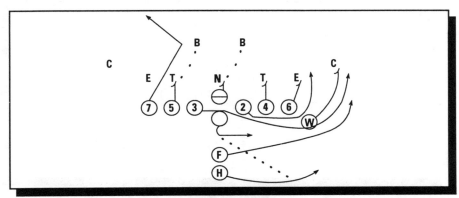

Diagram 12-29

√ We also like to add the "switch" call off the base scheme. For example, I Right 58 Sweep Base Switch (Diagram 12-30).

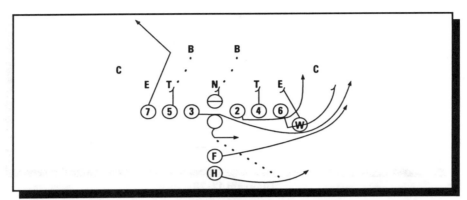

Diagram 12-30

Coaching Point: As was previously discussed, the "switch" call tells the wing to block down and the tight end to pull and base.

b. I Right 58 Sweep Base vs. the 43 defense (Diagram 12-31).

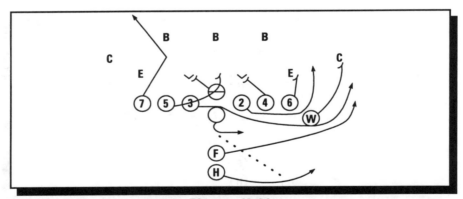

Diagram 12-31

c. I Right 58 Sweep Base vs. the Split defense (Diagram 12-32).

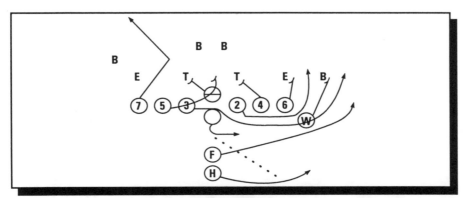

Diagram 12-32

d. I Right 58 Sweep Base vs. the Eagle defense (Diagram 12-33).

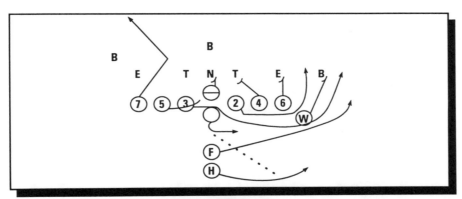

Diagram 12-33

Carl O. "Bill" Gentry was born in Slaton, Texas in 1926. Following graduation from Slaton High School, he served in the United States Navy during World War II.

After his service in the Navy, Bill attended Coffeyville Junior College in Coffeyville, Kansas for two years. He then attended the University of New Mexico in Albuquerque, New Mexico from which he graduated with B.S. and M.S. degrees.

In 1958 Bill became the head football coach at Highland High School in Albuquerque, New Mexico. After 31 years at Highland, Bill left Highland to become the head football coach at Eldorado High School in Albuquerque before the 1989 season. Bill spent seven years at Eldorado, before retiring after the 1995 season.

In almost four decades as a head coach, Bill's overall record was 305-102-5. His teams averaged winning eight games per year for 38 years. His teams appeared in the state finals ten times, winning the New Mexico state championship three times.

In recognition of his extraordinary accomplishments, Coach Gentry was named National High School Football Coach of the Year in 1994 by the National High School Athletic Coaches Association. He has also been inducted into the Albuquerque Sports Hall of Fame, the New Mexico High School Athletic Coaches Association Hall of Honor and the University of New Mexico Lobo Hall of Honor.

Currently, Bill lives in Albuquerque, New Mexico, with his wife of 46 years, Mary. In his leisure time, Bill likes walking, camping, trout fishing, and bird hunting.

ADDITIONAL FOOTBALL RESOURCES FROM

COACHES CHOICE

■ *COACHING LINEBACKERS*
by Jerry Sandusky and Cedric X. Bryant
1996 ▪Paper▪ 136 pp
ISBN 1-57167-059-9 ▪ $15.00

■ *COACHING OFFENSIVE BACKS*
by Steve Axman
1997 ▪Paper▪ 230 pp
ISBN 1-57167-088-2 ▪ $19.00

■ *DEVELOPING AN OFFENSIVE GAME PLAN*
by Brian Billick
1997 ▪Paper▪ 102 pp
ISBN 1-57167-046-7 ▪ $15.00

■ *101 LINEBACKER DRILLS*
by Jerry Sandusky and Cedric X. Bryant
1997 ▪Paper▪ 120 pp▪ $15.00
ISBN 1-57167-087-4